THE NIGHT OF THE WICKED WINDS

Books by Roger Pickenpaugh

A History of Noble County, Ohio, 1887-1987
Noble County Vistas
Rescue by Rail
Savage Skies
Blizzard of the Century
Buckeye Blizzard
River on a Rampage
The Night of the Wicked Winds

Cover Photos:
Front: Upside down piano in the debris of a church along Route 257, Delaware County. *(Gladys Geesey)*
Back: Damaged car in Seneca County. *(Donna Fox and Larry T. Egbert)*

THE NIGHT OF THE WICKED WINDS

THE 1965 PALM SUNDAY TORNADOES IN OHIO

ROGER PICKENPAUGH

GATEWAY PRESS, INC.
Baltimore, MD   2003

Copyright © 2003 by
Roger Pickenpaugh
All rights reserved.

Permission to reproduce in any form
must be secured from the author.

Please direct all correspondence and book orders to:
Roger Pickenpaugh
501 Oaklawn
Caldwell, OH 43724

Library of Congress Control Number 2003102761
ISBN 0-9709059-3-9

Published for the author by
Gateway Press, Inc.
1001 N. Calvert Street
Baltimore, MD 21202-3897

Printed in the United States of America

**To Anya,
with love**

Roger Pickenpaugh is a journalism and history teacher at Shenandoah Elementary School in Noble County Ohio. His previous books include *Rescue by Rail: Troop Transfer and the Civil War in the West, 1863* (University of Nebraska Press, 1998)

He is pictured with the staff of the *Gazette*, the SES student newspaper, a group he calls "a talented group of writers and a treasured group of friends."
Left to right: Heather Warner, Emily Reed, Hannah Hall, Samantha Crum, Josh Cowgill, Kelsey Bond, Hannah Rich, Rachel Bridgman, Devon Smith, Annie Scott, Rachel Sorg, Hannah Guy, Spencer Wise, Zak Gress, Jacob Parks, Andy Bauknecht, Drew West, Ethan Williams, Charles Bragg.

Contents

Preface	viii
1. "Death Whirled from the Sky"	1
2. Hoosier Invader	16
3. "Dad, Outside the Window Is a T…"	27
4. Toledo's Tornado	46
5. "Then, All of a Sudden, KABOOM!"	59
6. "Did You Say a Church Stood There?"	76
7. Scattered Storms, Scattered Lives	102
Notes	109
Bibliography	114
Index	118

Preface

"Was that the tornado that hit Xenia?"

It was the most common response I got when I told people I was writing a book about the 1965 Palm Sunday Tornadoes. It's understandable. The storm that devastated Xenia April 3, 1974, was a benchmark tragedy, an event that deserves to be remembered.

It is unfortunate, however, that Xenia's tornado has tended to overshadow so thoroughly other episodes in Ohio's weather history. One of the goals of this book is to remind Buckeye State residents that other significant tornadoes have taken place here, bringing their share of death and destruction. Several of them occurred on April 11, 1965.

A number of people have helped me do that. As with all my other weather related books, my greatest debt is to the many people who shared their stories with me. If this book is boring, it has to be my fault, because those stories were anything but. If some areas seem to get more coverage than others, it is simply because more people came forward in certain communities than in others. People's names appear as they requested, and their stories appear as they were told.

Although I do not wish to dwell on it, it seemed that I ran across more uncooperative people in researching this book than any previous one. For example, I drove the two hours to Delaware County to interview Farmer L. When I called his home at our agreed upon time, there was no answer. The same was true an hour later. When I called a few weeks later to try again, he said it was harvest time and I had missed my "window of opportunity" to talk to him. Mrs. K. in Van Wert County not only refused to be interviewed but basically accused me of being a crook. A Toledo "lady" sent an email message well garnished with advice on how to write the book. She also said she had a story. When I tried to set up a time for an interview, she said she was afraid to meet me in person; she would talk on the phone, later. When I called later, she said she would email me her story. She never did. Mr. L. in Lorain County said he had covered the tornadoes for a local newspaper. I called many times, but he always had some reason for not being able to talk (one night it was a ball game on TV). Finally I set up a definite time on a Saturday morning. When I called there was no answer. My point here is not so much to complain about those morons (well, maybe a little) but to explain that they make me appreciate my sources all the more.

Early in the research phase of this project, I ran into Debbie Watters. At the time I planned on including Indiana stories in this book, and I was visiting the Hoosier State searching for sources. I learned that Debbie had the same idea in mind, and considering her personal involvement in the tragedy, she certainly had a claim to the Hoosier State's experiences. I appreciate her help with my work, and I hope I have been some help to her. If you find the stories in this book interesting, I would urge you to look for her forthcoming book. Anyone having Indiana stories can contact her at the *Tipton Tribune* at 765-675-2115.

Several newspapers ran my appeals for sources, a huge help. Among those helping out were Paul Morton, *Oberlin News-Tribune*; Connie Davis, *Elyria Chronicle-Telegram*; Angela Mitro, Herald Newspapers of Toledo; Ron Simon, *Mansfield News-Journal*; and Mike Lackey, *Lima News*. To those individuals and newspapers inadvertently left out, I apologize. To all I am grateful.

I am also grateful to all those who shared photographs. Sources are cited with the photos, but I would also like to thank Elmer Turner of the Cleveland Public Library and fellow patron Julia Sivertson, who helped me in the process of copying the photos there. Matilda Phlipot of the Shelby County Historical Society located an excellent set of slides and made them available free of charge. Only the Allen County Historical Society, which asked for what I considered a ridiculously steep fee, proved less than cooperative. As always, the staff of the Ohio Historical Society was helpful when I went to Columbus to track down newspaper sources.

Dave Arbenz, colleague at the Shenandoah Elementary School, once again waded through my prose and once again made it better. Author and historian Gary Williams also did both. Several of my friends on the staff of the *Gazette*, Shenandoah's excellent school newspaper, helped with the proofreading as well. One of them, Annie Scott, also helped assemble the index.

This book is my seventh with Gateway Press of Baltimore. It will not, I hope, be the last. Publisher Anne Hughes has guided me through every one of them over the course of the last fifteen years. A much anticipated trip to Baltimore to see a good friend is always one of the greatest rewards of a completed manuscript.

As always, the support and assistance of family was invaluable. My parents, Les and Fern Pickenpaugh, copied and developed the photographs for this book, and helped with the mail orders.

Marion, as always, made everything come together. It would take up several pages to list everything she did. Instead, I'll focus on two. One, she wrote down and alphabetized every entry for the index, a thanklessly mundane but essential task. Second, and even more important, she put up with me as I went through that bizarre process known as writing a book. Anyone who has ever written or endured someone who has written knows what I mean.

1

"Death Whirled from the Sky"

Iowa, Wisconsin, & Illinois

April 11, 1965, was a balmy day in Ohio and much of the American Midwest, unseasonably so. The first warm weekend day of the year, it brought many residents of the Buckeye State out of their homes for spring chores or simply to enjoy the afternoon's hopeful hint that another winter was over. As they ventured out their doors Ohioans had no way of knowing that a deadly storm system was brewing to the west. Indeed, it had already begun. Early that afternoon a tornado touched down in Cedar County Iowa, the first of at least thirty-seven that would strike a six-state area that day. It left one man fatally injured, the first of 258 to die in what was to become one of America's deadliest tornado outbreaks.

The Iowa tornado moved northeast from Cedar County into Clinton and Jackson Counties. Twenty-five farms lay in its path, and many were extensively damaged by winds that students of the tornadoes would later place at F4, a level of winds described as "catastrophic" on the Fujita Scale of tornado intensity. The sole fatality was a man caught by the storm as he attempted to reach a storm cellar. United Press International reported that the twister lifted his home fifty to sixty feet into the air before hurling it back to the ground, burying him in the debris. He died several weeks later.[1]

As the system traveled east, Wisconsin and Illinois were the next states in line. Seven significant tornadoes hit Wisconsin, killing three people and injuring eighty-four. The three Wisconsin deaths occurred near Watertown in Jefferson County. All of the victims had been in automobiles thrown from the highway. A trucker whose semi trailer was picked up on Interstate 94 told a reporter, "It was a bundle of rain with a wildcat in it. I was so scared," he said, "that I was sick." One Watertown resident called his wife to the basement as the tornado approached and watched his home "disappear above her as she descended." In the Green County community of Monroe, twenty-five injured people were taken to a local hospital, where a call went out for all available surgeons. Over sixty homes and fifty businesses there were damaged or destroyed, as were buildings on twenty-seven surrounding farms.[2]

In Illinois at least three tornadoes struck. One was responsible for six deaths and seventy-five injuries. Five people were killed in the Chicago suburb of Crystal Lake. A waitress told the *Chicago Tribune* that she looked out the window of the lounge where she was working toward a shopping center across the street and saw "roofs... peeling off like paper and cars in the parking lot... being tossed around." One of the cars crashed through the window of a nearby laundromat. The tornado leveled fifteen homes in the community and damaged hundreds more. Tower officials at O'Hare International Airport sighted a funnel cloud fifteen miles to the west. It never touched down, but high winds blew a single-engine plane some one hundred feet.[3]

Indiana

The storms intensified in strength and increased in numbers as they blew into Indiana. The Hoosier State suffered 180 deaths and over 1,600 injuries as ten major tornadoes struck between 5:45 and 9:00 p.m. All hit in the northern half of the state, devastating numerous communities and overwhelming emergency responders. Soon after the storms had passed, a state police officer told the Associated Press, "They can't even make an estimate on the number of injured. They're just hauling them away, load after load." The southernmost Indiana twister cut a forty-five mile swath through Montgomery, Boone, and Hamilton Counties, leaving twenty-eight dead and 123 injured. North of Lebanon the damage path was a mile wide. Fifty-four homes were destroyed in the area, and eleven people died. Ten more were killed further to the northeast near Sheridan. Among them were six persons representing three generations of one family.[4]

At the same time another tornado was touching down about twenty miles to the north in Howard County. It would continue into Grant County, leaving in its wake F4 damage, twenty-five deaths, and over 800 injuries. The first community in the storm's path was Russiaville, where it left three people dead, one an eight-year old boy, whose body was found on a lawn between two houses. "Like a city that has been bombed and burned," was one National Guardsman's description of the small village. Palm Sunday services were being conducted in three Russiaville churches when the storm hit at about 7:25. In two of them the congregations had time to get to the basement. At the third, the Baptist Church, the pastor shouted for his fifty-two parishioners to drop to the floor. The building collapsed, and the floor dropped partially into the basement. Four persons were trapped briefly, but the solid wooden pews afforded protection, and no one was seriously hurt. Ironically, the lack of time to head to the basement likely saved many from being crushed.

"Alto," reported the *Kokomo Times*, "is no more." Where the tiny community's store and school had been, as well as a number of homes, "there is almost nothing but rubble," the paper added. Still, Alto was lucky. Nobody died. Kokomo was also spared any deaths as the tornado ripped through the Maple Crest suburb, destroying homes, businesses, and an apartment complex. Greentown was much less fortunate, as the storm "left a path of nothing but splintered boards and household goods" along the south side of U. S. Route 35, leaving ten people dead. Still, there were remarkable stories of survival. A family of three took shelter in a closet. When they emerged it was the only part of their house still standing. The same was true of a man and his son who lay on a hallway floor, and a family that took shelter in a bathroom. Yet another family headed for the garage and got in their automobile. Their house and the garage that surrounded them were blown away, but the car was untouched. Grant County suffered five deaths, three near the town of Swayzee. Twenty were injured when the tornado unroofed a portion of a Veterans Administration hospital near Marion.[5]

In extreme northern Indiana four tornadoes killed seventy people in Starke, Marshall, St. Joseph, Elkhart, and La Grange Counties. Over 700 were hurt. Elkhart County was in the path of all four storms, and there the death toll reached fifty-four. Ten deaths occurred at the Midway Trailer Court, a mobile home park at Dunlap, a short distance southeast of Elkhart. Eighty of the ninety-four mobile homes there were destroyed. The *New York Times* reported that the wing of an airplane parked nearby was found six miles away. Elkhart County Sheriff Woody L. Caton was among the first on the scene. "Everything there was a mess-- completely flattened," he later told the *Elkhart Truth*. The sheriff and volunteers began searching for victims, finding "three dead right where we started." Soon, Caton later recalled, "People were coming out of their basements and they were staggering toward me. They had blood and dirt on their faces and couldn't see." All the sheriff could do was tell them to "hold onto the car until help came. At one time," he noted, "I had about six people clinging to the car."[6]

Multiple deaths were common in Elkhart and La Grange Counties. Fourteen locations were responsible for a total of forty-three deaths, and the Midway Trailer Park was the scene of the worst of them. There six members of one family died in their mobile home, both parents and four children ranging in age from one to five years. At a nearby trailer a mother and her six-month old son were killed.

Just north of the Midway Trailer Court, the Sunnyside Housing Addition was the site of four multiple deaths. Married couples were killed in all four cases, and in two, a child also died. Twenty-eight people lost their lives in Sunnyside and the nearby Kingston Heights development. Among them was ten-year old Steve Forsythe. In 1995 Steve's sister, Debbie (Forsythe) Watters, wrote down her memories of that night. "I can't believe," she wrote, "it has been thirty years since the sky turned black and death whirled from the sky." Charles "Chuck" and Shirley Forsythe, along with Steve, Debbie, and eleven-year old Mike, had spent that afternoon at the New Paris Speedway, where Chuck was a flagman. A hard rain began to fall as they headed home. "By the time we reached our house," Debbie recalled, "the wind was picking up and it was hailing." Mike left with friends to attend a church service. The rest of the Forsythe family planned to stay home that evening.

That changed when Chuck's fire radio crackled with the message that a tornado had hit the Midway Trailer Court. The volunteer fireman was quickly "on his way to help all he could." About twenty minutes later Mike called to ask for a ride home; the storms, he explained, had canceled the service. As his mother informed him that his father had taken the car, Steve interrupted. "Mom!" he shouted, "There is one coming here!" The television had issued the warning that a tornado was headed toward Sunnyside. Shirley glanced out a window, then shouted, "Oh my God! Kids, get to the basement!" The trio huddled together, watching through a basement window as their neighbors' home blew away. Debbie whispered to herself, "Goodbye, Stevie," but said nothing to her mother. "A couple seconds later," Debbie wrote, "it sounded as if a freight train was going right over us. It was the loudest, most distinct sound I had ever heard." Debbie was ripped from her mother's arms, and "dirt and mud were flying around just as fast as the tornado itself," and toward the end she heard her brother call for his mother, and then there was a loud crash followed by silence "as calm as if nothing had ever happened."

It was over. "I opened my eyes," Debbie recalled, "and started crying, saying, 'Mommy, Mommy.'"

Then she heard a whirling noise overhead and looked up to see a two-by-four "coming straight at me." She ducked, but the board hit hard on the top of her head. After two unsuccessful attempts, Debbie managed to stand up. She saw her mother lying on the floor and the family dog "wobbling through what used to be our front porch." She could not find Steve at first. Then, after moving a cinder block, "I saw Stevie's legs mostly buried in the rubble." Debbie froze, fully aware that she had lost her brother. She moved toward her mother, who "looked like someone had beaten her with a bat. There was mud and blood all over her." Still, Shirley Forsythe managed to stand up and walk free from the rubble that had been her home. She was incoherent, however, and walked straight toward a ditch with a live downed wire in it. A man yelled, Debbie grabbed her mother, and the good Samaritan jumped over the wire and carried Shirley to his car. An ambulance arrived, but it was so crowded with victims that Debbie and Shirley had to sit in the front seat. As they rode to the hospital, Mrs. Forsythe groaned in pain.

They had no way of knowing that, as they departed, Chuck Forsythe was racing for home in his fire truck. He had seen the tornado bearing down on the neighborhood, and he arrived just as the ambulance pulled out. For him and Mike, it was the start of forty-eight hours of terrifying uncertainty. He found Steve quickly. The family dog was lying over his body as if to protect him. Chuck knew Mike had gone with friends, but he had no idea where his wife and daughter were. His fellow firefighters soon arrived and removed him from the scene.

Meanwhile Shirley had been transferred to Memorial Hospital in South Bend. She was cut extensively. One cut was so deep and so full of dirt and wood that doctors did not expect her to live. A nurse told her that Steve was in the hospital and doing well, and with that she drifted off to sleep. Debbie was placed in a rollaway bed in a corridor of the crowded hospital. There were curlers in her hair, she remembered, "twisted and matted with blood and mud." A nurse had to shave her head just to ascertain the extent of her injuries. She was taken to surgery, awaking in a baby crib. Debbie had thirty-seven stitches in her head, stretching from ear to ear. "I just remember getting visitors who always looked like they wanted to cry," is about all she would recall of her hospitalization. The happiest event of her stay occurred the next morning, when her father arrived. She leapt to his arms, but Chuck, worried about his daughter's condition, gently placed her back down. She told him Steve was dead. "I know, baby," her father replied.

What Chuck Forsythe still did not know was where his wife was-- or even if she was still alive. With family members and friends, he had spent the night searching hospitals and morgues. Finding Debbie had been the first bright spot. He left and headed to Memorial Hospital, the last facility left, with little hope. Finding Shirley was a tremendous relief, but Chuck still faced overwhelming responsibilities. Toughest among them was telling Mike he had lost his brother and Shirley that she had lost her son. He had funeral arrangements to make and a wife and a daughter still hospitalized. On top of that, he had no idea where his family was going to live.

Steve's funeral was the ironic site of the Forsythe family's reunion. The hospital let Shirley out just long enough for the service. She sat in a wheelchair, "her head still bloody and wrapped in bandages." She saw Debbie and said, "There's my baby!" then began to cry. Months of plastic surgery lay ahead for Mrs. Forsythe, but her physical wounds healed, and at the time of this writing, she and Chuck are still living in Indiana. The family rebuilt about two miles from Sunnyside, "but with an empty spot," Debbie emphasizes, "that could never be filled." Storms still scare Debbie, but not as badly as they did during the years immediately following the tornado. "If it started to lightning and thunder," she recorded, "I was in tears. If there were storm warnings, I was hysterical."[7]

6   *The Night of the Wicked Winds*

Russiaville, Indiana, took a direct hit from the tornado. (Kokomo Times)

A school bus peeks from the wreckage west of Alto, Indiana. (Kokomo Times)

Very little was left of Alto, Indiana. (Kokomo Times)

Michigan

As Indiana's deadly tornadoes lifted, ten twisters descended on Michigan. They were widely scattered, and most had a relatively short path, at least compared to those in other states. Five did not result in a single death and produced only seven injuries between them. Two of the storms killed one person each. However, an F4 tornado that struck Ottawa and Kent Counties left five people dead just north of Grand Rapids. The storm produced 142 injuries. Among them was the sheriff of Grand Traverse County, who had been passing through on business. "The wind came whistling-- a very shrill whistle-- like an old German 88 shell in World War II," said Sheriff Richard Weiler from a hospital bed in Grand Rapids. He suffered "a severe leg injury," according to press accounts when he and some fifty patrons of a restaurant were trapped in debris. At another restaurant a trucker reported that the cab of his tractor-trailer was "smashed against the building and ruined." The man had sought shelter in a corner of the room when two large windows blew out. Although unhurt, he quickly added, "If I live to be a hundred I don't want to go through anything like this again." Neither did the injured. One emergency room doctor said of his patients, "Just about all of them looked like they were tattooed with sand. It was just driven into the skin." Virtually all had cuts and bruises. A few suffered multiple fractures. In the midst of the tragedy some found humor when a semi-trailer overturned, spilling its load of baby food. On the rear door of the trailer was a sign advising, "Litter costs you tax $$$."[8]

The deadliest storm of the entire outbreak devastated sections of Branch, Hillsdale, Lenawee, and Monroe Counties in southern Michigan. It left forty-four dead and over 600 injured. The storm began in extreme northeastern Indiana, but virtually all of the damage path and all of the deaths took place in Michigan. There were actually two tornadoes, occurring about one-half hour apart, but their paths were virtually identical. In many places the second twister struck as rescuers arrived and dazed victims emerged in the wake of the first. In one case a would-be rescuer in Hillsdale County was killed by a falling tree during the second tornado. In another situation, a couple whose home had been destroyed by the first twister sought shelter with neighbors. They were making sleeping arrangements when the second tornado destroyed that home. Branch County was hit first, and it was hit hard. At least nineteen people died, and some two hundred were injured. Damage was extensive in the village of East Gilead and along Coldwater Lake. The winds scattered debris across the lake.[9]

Next in line was Hillsdale County. There the tornado leveled a home north of Reading. Two boys, ages two and three, were killed after the tornado blew them from their father's arms. The younger boy's body was found two hours later, several hundred yards from the home site. From there the storms roared to Bear Lake, destroying several homes. One was a brand new house on the lake shore. "What's left of it is up here on the ridge," the owner told the *Hillsdale Daily News*. For one *News* employee the story was personal. His home was demolished, but his wife, children, and visiting relatives reached the basement in time. Another couple returned from a weekend trip to discover only the foundation of their house remaining.[10]

Fred Sprang, who lived at Bear Lake, remembers "hearing that terrible roar." It was still daylight, and he looked out the window of his home and saw the funnel coming. There was no basement in their cement block home, so Sprang hustled his wife, Carolyn, and daughters Sandra and Sarah to the car. Carolyn was four months pregnant, and as she tried to enter through the driver's side, she became stuck under the steering wheel. Sandra (Sprang) Compton recalls watching her father push Carolyn through then looking out the back window and seeing a "white tornado." As he pulled out Fred looked in the rear view mirror and saw part of their home blow away and another building flying across the road. The family headed north, but the car did not perform well. There was not enough oxygen in the air, Fred feels, for it to run correctly. Rocks and branches struck the vehicle, and at one point the wind lifted it a few feet off the ground. Limbs from a recently cut walnut tree bounced down the road, and the car came down on top of one of them, bending the wheels and removing the exhaust system.

Remains of the Fred Sprang home, Hillsdale, Michigan. (Sandra Compton)

Fleeing in a car as a tornado approaches is not generally accepted advice, but in this case it seemed to be the proper course. The Sprang home was destroyed, and Sandra's and Sarah's beds each had three cement blocks lying on them. The storm removed mortar from between several blocks and deposited the blocks back as they had been. A piece of straw was driven through the wood of the family's electric organ. When they took the instrument to be repaired, three pounds of gold carpet were found in it. The family never learned to whom the carpet belonged.

Sprang was a deputy with the Hillsdale County Sheriff's Department. He took his family to a neighbor's home and began three consecutive days on the job. The Salvation Army and the Red Cross set up a canteen for rescue workers, and Sprang notes, "I never ate so many Spam sandwiches in my life." Preventing looting was one of his main challenges, but the task was virtually impossible. There was "a lot of theft" he recalls. Even the deputy himself was a victim. At one point he put down his radio to help remove a tree limb from a car. When he returned it was gone. Much more disheartening was the search for bodies. Sprang found one victim who had been blown from his home. The man's feet plowed a deep furrow into the ground.[11]

The bus that Fred Sprang drove for the Hillsdale Schools. (Sandra Compton)

Another rescuer and victim was Greg Ross, a Hillsdale resident, who had spent Palm Sunday morning washing and waxing his 1962 Corvette. That evening he took the rags to the laundromat. While there two customers received calls informing them that their homes had been hit by a tornado. At least one, he heard, lived at Bear Lake. He picked up a friend, Dennis Trevathan, and the pair headed toward Bear Lake in Ross's shiny Corvette to see if they could help. They encountered fallen trees and flattened homes in the small community of Bankers. Then they glanced west and saw that they were about to encounter "a solid front of thunderstorms." The pair came to a stop, looked back, and saw the funnel of the second tornado. A stone farm house sat to their right, but at that point it didn't matter. The car was being moved, and Ross had the feeling of "being a piece on a Ouija board." Objects bounced off the windshield, and a tree stump took off a fender of the recently polished Corvette.

The funnel passed directly over the car, bringing an instant of calm. Ross looked directly up into it, and it was, he says, "one of the most beautiful things I've ever seen." Rain, he adds, refracted the light from flashes of lightning, producing "every color of the rainbow." His car was rather less beautiful. A tree had struck the trunk, and Ross and Trevathan climbed through limbs to get out. The stone farm house was virtually gone. The pair went to see if they could help, dodging golf ball-size hail stones as they did. As they approached the remains of the house the storm cellar door opened, and the owner invited them in. They remained briefly then returned to the road to help a couple whose car had struck a downed tree. A second car appeared, and the driver took the injured couple plus Ross and Trevathan to the hospital in Hillsdale. From there the two friends returned to their homes. Later that evening they went to the sheriff's department to offer their services. They were sent back to the Bankers area, along with a third friend, Darrel Scharp. The three helped cut a path through for emergency vehicles, searched the remains of homes for victims, and located two families of disoriented victims and got them to safety. After that, Scharp recalls, they went to North Adams, where a barn had collapsed on a herd of cattle. Many, he says, had to be destroyed.

The group's next assignment, which came at about 2:00 a.m., sent them to State Route 34 in the area of Madden Hills. A woman was brought to the Hillsdale hospital after being blown from her car. All she could say was, "My husband's in the car." She repeated it over and over. The three were sent to search for him. Scharp and Ross remember the details differently, but according to Ross, the search took them to a tree line around Baw Beese Lake. They came to a spot "that looked like something went through it." Following it they found "what was left of the car." It had flown at least twenty feet through the trees, shearing off their tops. Retracing their steps, Ross says, he tripped over the body of the victim. Other duties for the trio included clearing roads of limbs and searching for victims along Ash-Te-Wette Road. "Everybody worked together," Scharp says of the marathon effort. "There were no classes."[12]

After the tornadoes struck, a lack of advance warning was suggested as a reason for the large number of deaths. At least one resident of Hillsdale County had a unique warning system. Kenneth Coe was sitting in his yard with friends and family members that Palm Sunday afternoon celebrating his wife's birthday. As they visited, Coe's German shepherd dog "came up to each of us and laid her head on our laps, looked at us and whined. She had never acted this way before," Coe continues, "especially to people she did not know." The last time he had seen a dog behave in that manner, he told his guests, was in the 1930s at his family's farm near Ypsilanti. The family dog, which was never allowed in the house, sneaked in and crawled under a bed. Coe's sister had to use a broom to dislodge him from the hiding place. Later that day a tornado had blown down one of their silos and knocked the barn off the foundation. Now, some three decades later, history repeated itself, although the 1965 tornadoes hit some four miles north of the Coe home.[13]

Southeast of Hillsdale, the tornado destroyed several homes at Baw Beese Lake. One belonged to an eighty-year old woman who was blown, along with the remains of her home, into the lake. She had been writing a letter when the storm hit. "I got a bump on the head," she told the *News*. "I may have been unconscious for a few minutes." She thought she was in her front yard, "but then I felt water," she related. The lady managed to drag herself to a piece of floating debris and began shouting for help. After some time, two neighbors, who had been surveying the damage to their homes, heard her. "Keep calling, lady," one yelled, "we'll find you." They did, pulling her to safety. She was about 700 feet downshore from where her house had been. After a brief time in the hospital, the lady went to stay with a nephew. She was there when she told the newspaper, "And they thought I had a bad heart."[14]

Daniel Watkins had returned to his home in Hillsdale from a date when he learned from a neighbor that the situation at Baw Beese Lake was serious. The parents of the neighbor's girl friend, who lived at the lake, needed a place to stay and were at his house. Watkins had been out of the army about a year, but he put his uniform back on and headed out to help. A deputy saw the uniform and let him through a roadblock. His very presence was immediately beneficial. Looters had already arrived, and he heard one whisper to a partner, "Hey, the National Guard's there. Let's get out of here." The entire area was "a total shambles," Watkins recalls. "I could recognize nothing." He did, however, locate the home of his neighbor's house guests, retrieving the man's glasses and wallet, as well as some needed medicine.[15]

John M. Fullerton also helped at Baw Beese Lake, assisting with the clean-up while home for spring break from Western Michigan University. He had been heading for Kalamazoo the night the tornadoes hit. He missed the storms but noticed the multi-colored sky, commenting to his traveling companion, "It looks like the world is coming to an end." Upon reaching the university he learned how accurate his assessment had been for many of the residents of his home county.[16]

Two people who realized that first hand were Dr. Philip B. Fleming, chief of anesthesia services at Hillsdale Community Health Center, and his wife Pat, a registered nurse at the facility. The cases at the hospital that night, the couple recalls, offered a variety of horrors. Fortunately many of the staff members were World War II veterans, and Dr. Fleming said the situation was "handled very well." Some victims, Pat says, were "so encrusted in mud we couldn't even see their injuries." They washed one woman's foot only to discover that a toe was missing. One patient was a pregnant woman upon whom a refrigerator had fallen. One fatality was a child whose body had been impaled by a two-by-four. In another case the state police brought in a man carrying a child whose head had been crushed. The child died at the hospital. Over 300 people were treated that night, straining the facility's two emergency rooms and one fracture room. The situation would have been worse were it not for the fact that many came from outlying areas, staggering the numbers arriving at a time. The doctor in charge of the emergency room had a home at Baw Beese Lake. He called his wife and learned that all was fine. A half hour later the physician was told to go home; the second tornado had taken his house. His wife survived by climbing into the fireplace.[17]

Michigan is a land of many lakes, and this tornado seemed to seek them out. In Lenawee County it was Devil's Lake, where the adjoining community of Manitou Beach was devastated. The damage included 263 houses and cottages destroyed and another 315 "damaged but livable," according to the *Adrian Telegram*. Fourteen businesses were destroyed and another fourteen damaged. Two churches and one school were destroyed, as were fifty farm buildings. The *Telegram* placed the damage at $3,534,500. A resident, whose home was destroyed, told the paper, "It is impossible to tell you what a person thinks about at a time like that. I heard a roar and dropped to the floor. Flying glass, debris, tree limbs, and junk came sailing through the house. It was a miracle that I escaped alive." Over 500 rescue workers were summoned to the area. One of them, a Marine Corps veteran of the South Pacific in World War II, said the destruction was "as complete as any bombardment he saw in his service career." Six members of one family were killed when the tornado leveled their home. A seventh member of the family, seventeen years old, had been working at a service station when the storm hit. He had no immediate family left. His parents, sister, brother-in-law, niece, and nephew were all gone.[18]

The churches destroyed were the St.-Mary's-on-the-Lake Catholic Church, and the Manitou Beach Bible Church, which had been dedicated the previous January. Sixty-five people had been attending services at the latter when the tornado struck. Twenty were rescued from the debris. One later died from his injuries. Barbara (Grubbs) Reyes should have been there that night, but her father, Harold Grubbs, decided to take Barbara and her sister, Carolyn, bowling instead. Her mother, Beverly, was working that night at a nearby restaurant. The storm started while they were bowling. When the power went out, the three returned home. By the time they got to Manitou Beach the first tornado had hit. They got to within six blocks of home then encountered roads blocked by debris. They went into a service station, where they heard the roar of the second twister approaching. All three lay on the floor, but the tornado missed the facility. From there they walked home. All of the windows were out of the Grubbs home, and a beam from their church, located one block away, had been blown through the girls' bedroom, striking their bunk beds. The storm had blown their dog through a window. They found the animal, alive and well, in the basement of a home across the street that had been destroyed. The girls stayed with their grandparents, who lived next door, while Mr. Grubbs walked two miles to check on Beverly. He found her safe at the restaurant, which the storm had not hit. The family fared relatively well. All were uninjured, and their house was less severely damaged than many. Their garage, which housed a trampoline business, was destroyed. Three or four of the trampolines were found in Devil's Lake, a mile away.[19]

The *Telegram* reported that eleven houses were damaged in the village of Onsted "with ten livable." The one that wasn't belonged to Fred and Geraldine Gibbs, who lived there with Geraldine's three daughters, Ruth, Violet, and Beverly. Violet Waltz recalls that her stepfather, sensing bad weather, did not go to work that Palm Sunday. He instructed the girls not to leave the yard. The family's toy terrier, Tiny, also sensed the approaching storm, running in and out of the basement constantly. Then it began, rain at first followed by golf ball-size hail. The hail stopped, and wind and lightning replaced it. The family watched the storm from a kitchen window, witnessing a lightning strike on a neighbor's barn. After that everything grew suddenly and ominously quiet, and Fred ordered everyone to the basement. As they rushed downstairs, Violet says, the family spotted three funnels out the kitchen door. Two were touching down.

They made it to the basement with virtually no time to spare. Fred was the last down. An iron skillet struck him as he descended. Above, Violet says, the sound was like that of "a giant vacuum cleaner." The family heard glass breaking and boards creaking. Then all was quiet. They tried to exit the way they had come, but debris blocked the path. The way was clear, however, up steps leading to the yard. They exited to discover that one bedroom was all that was left standing of their home. Their car had been blown about thirty feet and turned 180 degrees, but there was "not a scratch on it." Downed power lines sparked all over the yard, and Fred told the children to stay put. The family would later learn that their cat and her new kittens were all killed, as were several chickens and rabbits. Fortunately a rental home they owned at Manitou Beach was among the few spared there. It would serve as the family's home for the next several years.[20]

The community of Tipton, located on Michigan Route 50, also sustained extensive damage. Every house in the town was at least slightly damaged, some losing their roofs. No one, however, was injured. Surrounding farm homes and buildings had varying degrees of damage. On one farm every building was blown down, and the house was severely damaged. Another home was ripped from its foundation, landing forty feet to the east. The couple living there had left twenty minutes before the storm hit.[21]

As will be noted several times in the pages that follow, the aftermath of the tornadoes witnessed the emergence of countless selfless individuals who assisted the victims. Among them was Clarence Heimerdinger, a seventy-two-year old dairy farmer, who lived near Clnton, Michigan. For three weeks, working without pay, Heimerdinger directed the work of volunteers in northeastern Lenawee County. By ten o'clock Monday morning he had rounded up his neighbors to begin the staggering task. They went first to a neighboring farm, where a dozen cows were buried, some still alive. The living ones were taken to Heimerdinger's farm to be milked. The crews then extricated farm machinery from the debris before moving on to the task of general clean-up. As they did, carloads of Farm Bureau members, service club representatives, and high school students joined in the effort. Heimerdinger's work earned him notice in the *Congressional Record*, which is still proudly in the possession of his daughter, Evelyn M. Gregg.[22]

The last of the Michigan tornadoes, an F2 storm that hit Tuscola County, producing neither death nor injury, touched down at about nine o'clock. Forty minutes earlier a much stronger twister had begun a fifty-five mile path of death and destruction across eastern Indiana and into Ohio. A night of wicked winds lay ahead for the Buckeye State. Before it was over fifty-nine Ohioans would die, over seven hundred would be injured, and countless lives would be changed forever. It was to be a night that would produce memories of tragedy and wonder, of terror and, in rare cases, humor. A few of those memories follow.

2

Hoosier Invader

Blackford, Wells, & Adams Counties Indiana

What was to become Ohio's first tornado of the Palm Sunday outbreak touched down in Blackford County Indiana at about 8:20 p.m. By the time it reached the Wells County village of Keystone it was a deadly F4 twister. Among its targets was the Keystone Friends Church, where twelve people were attending services. Wells County Coroner Robert Haggard told the *Bluffton News-Banner* that it was very hard to believe that all of them survived the destruction of the church. The structure had been flattened, Haggard reported, "no higher than an automobile." Two members of the congregation were hospitalized. More would have been had they not ducked quickly under the pews. A Keystone couple escaped death when their home "came crashing down upon them." They emerged from the wreckage by crawling over a hot overturned stove, then, covered with fuel oil and blood, walked over a mile before they flagged down a car for the trip to the hospital.

Less fortunate were Susan Harris and her nine-year old daughter, Deborah. Both were instantly killed by flying debris as they dashed for the safety of a well pit. It was their deaths that brought Coroner Haggard to Keystone.[1]

Samuel F. Cooper and his wife, Waneta, were neighbors of the Harris family. "I just didn't like the way things looked," Mrs. Cooper says of that evening. The radio told of impending storms, and she filled the oil lamps and got out some flashlights. A neighbor family of four came over, and everyone joined Samuel, who had been reloading shotgun shells, in the basement. One of the neighbors' daughters was ill. They had forgotten the child's blanket, so Waneta ran upstairs to find one. Glancing outside on her way, she saw the funnel about one-quarter of a mile away. She ran back down to the basement, and shouted, "Here it comes!" Samuel looked out a basement window as a four-by-four crashed through it, barely missing him.

After the tornado passed everyone returned upstairs to survey the damage. Glass was everywhere, and the drapes were flapping through the holes where the windows had been. Looking outside, Samuel and Waneta saw that their garage was gone, as was the Friends Church, located next door. (The pastor later told Waneta a gust of wind had lifted the church from the floor, and he instructed the congregation to get beneath the pews. A second gust, he added, rocked the structure, and a third destroyed it.) Later they heard someone at a back door. It was Mrs. Harris's husband and the couple's two sons, who had been visiting neighbors when the storm hit. He came in and collapsed, saying his wife was "hurt awful bad." Samuel and another man went and found the mangled bodies of Mrs. Harris and her daughter. The Cooper home, one of few standing in the neighborhood, became a clearing house for several homeless storm victims, including some with injuries. They remained until ambulances could get past downed trees.[2]

Three miles north of Keystone, Alice Ann Norris Van Wagner and her husband, Alfred Norris, returned home early from church services in Bluffton, Indiana, when Alice suddenly went into labor. "It was pitch black and raining," Alice says of their eight-mile trip home. Along the way Alfred dodged boards, insulation, limbs, and other debris from the damage path of the tornado. They called their Bluffton doctor, who told them not to come yet; the community was experiencing a terrible storm. Per his instructions, they waited until the contractions were three minutes apart. They arrived at a hospital with "policemen and flashing police cars everywhere." An officer approached their car but yielded when he saw Alice's obvious condition. In the labor room both Alfred and the doctor listened to radio accounts of the storms. At 1:32 a.m., April 12, Betsy Annette Norris "came into a stormy world." Her father would later say that she had been "a tornado ever since being born!"[3]

Continuing east, the twister crossed into Adams County. There it would revive memories of another Palm Sunday tornado. The earlier storm had occurred on March 28, 1920, killing five. The 1965 storm killed two people, one in and one near the small village of Linn Grove. At their family's farm, southwest of the town, Melissa (Grandlienard) Fey and her sister, Judy, were watching the Ed Sullivan Show. Jerry and the Pacemakers were scheduled to perform on the program, and Melissa recalls being disappointed when the power went off before they appeared. Their parents, Dale and Izzy, quickly herded the girls to the basement. Their mother went with them, but Dale remained at the top of the stairs to watch the approaching funnel. He stayed until the tornado was close-- too close. When Mr. Grandlienard attempted to head downstairs, the suction of the tornado made it impossible to open the cellar door. Mother and daughters waited out the storm for what "seemed like a lifetime," Melissa recalls. "Not only was our house being torn apart, but where was our father?"

Finally Dale came down to get them. They walked outside and looked up in wonder at a sky glistening with stars. Their barn was gone, as were all the outbuildings on the farm. The wind had torn the roof off their house and largely cleaned out the attic below it. Melissa's brother, Steve, had an old truck missing an engine he was in the process of restoring. The tornado dragged it some 300 feet, leaving tire marks along its path. Steve had been at the movies when the storm hit. Downed power lines greatly delayed his trip home. After briefly surveying the damage, Melissa says, "We sat alone in the dark on our porch, wondering what to do." They eventually went to stay with an aunt and uncle. The couple lived less that a mile away, but the storm had missed them. Their power had not even been disrupted. The Grandlienards remained there the following week, waiting for the electricity to be restored to their home. They moved back into their damaged house but rebuilt outward, removing the second story. Curious onlookers annoyed them and their neighbors during the clean-up process. Melissa recalls that one neighbor nailed a two-by-four to a tree, making it appear to the onlookers that the board had been blown through it.[4]

Linn Grove took a direct hit. As the storm approached the community it claimed its first Adams County victim, a man trying to escape the tornado in his pickup truck. The funnel overtook him, and his body was recovered the next morning some distance from the vehicle. His wife chose to remain in the basement of their home. The house was lost, but she survived. The other death occurred in the village itself, when a mobile home was blown into the debris of one of the village's two churches. The lone occupant, a seventy-eight-year old man, suffered a fractured skull. A reporter from the *Berne Witness*, who surveyed the wreckage, wrote that, "Fully sixty to seventy percent of the town is gone," including both churches. The town's hardware store and its grocery store-post office were both badly damaged.[5]

For Linn Grove residents John F. and Judy Habegger, April 11 had been a typical Sunday. Church, lunch, and a visit to Judy's parents' home with daughter Dawn, then two, had largely composed the day. Still, John recalls, "It just did not seem like a normal day." There was "a stillness in the afternoon," with no birds singing and a greenish yellow color to the sky. Heading for home at about eight that evening, clouds were gathering. As they got to the house the wind was picking up. Their home, built on a slab, had no basement, and John thought if the weather got worse the family would go to the brick church next door. The storm hit suddenly, however, and there was no time. Watching the huge cloud approach, Judy momentarily froze. Breaking windows startled her. Meanwhile John snatched Dawn from her crib. He and Judy lay on the floor, John covering his daughter.

According to John, the oft-repeated, "It sounds like a freight train," is "an adequate description." He held Dawn tightly, but the tornado's suction still yanked her from his arms. "The entire house lifted up and over us," he recalls. John and Judy rolled and were deposited in their front yard. "It reminds you of a tire," Judy says of the experience. John remembers the feeling of "exposed skin being peppered with debris" and the wind removing his shoes. Despite the ordeal, both were unhurt, and they immediately began moving debris, trying, without success, to locate Dawn. The Habeggers checked on a neighbor couple, who were also uninjured, and as they returned to their yard heard a "faint muffled cry." It was Dawn, lying in a field some fifty to sixty feet away from their home site. Debris surrounded her, Judy says, but she was in "a cleared space, like God had taken the ground and wiped the whole space clean." That she was injured was painfully clear, but the extent of her injuries was not. Their car was smashed, and the roads were blocked, and it would be nearly an hour before an ambulance arrived. John and Judy took their daughter to a nearby parsonage, washed the mud out of her mouth with cold coffee, and did all they could to keep her conscious. As they waited, John and the pastor toured the village, seeing if anybody required any assistance. They also recovered the body of the man whose trailer had been blown into the church wreckage.

The experience had been, in a literal sense, numbing. At one point Judy stepped on a nail sticking out of a board. "I just pulled it out," she recalls, "and barely felt a thing." The injury would nevertheless result in an overnight stay at the Bluffton clinic. For Dawn the clinic visit would be considerably longer. She was admitted with a skull fracture, cuts, bruises, and punctures. A piece of straw had been driven into her head. Doctors later told John and Judy that they did not send her on to a Fort Wayne hospital because they did not expect her to live through the night. Some four weeks later she was home.

Home, however, did not exist. The only item still affixed to the slab of the house was one toilet stool. The lid, John remembers, was still attached and functioning, but the seat was gone. Their stove was never found. One of their wedding pictures was found, however, by someone in Findlay, Ohio. Otherwise only a few pieces of furniture could be salvaged. A two-by-six driven into the yard at a forty-five degree angle could not be removed. John dug two feet into the ground, still could not budge it, and finally cut it off. Next door a delivery truck was suspended high enough in a maple tree that one could walk under it.

And still, through it all, the Habeggers felt fortunate, indeed even blessed. "Material things do not make a family," John asserts. "The three of us I feel are modern day miracles," he continues, "protected by the hand of God." With debris flying like missiles everywhere, "to be picked up bodily and protected was not just luck."[6]

As the tornado traveled slightly north of east from Linn Grove, heading toward the town of Berne, it struck a number of homes. At one a birthday party was being held. The house was destroyed, and sixteen of the eighteen party goers were hospitalized.[7] A birthday party had also taken place that day at the home of Tom and Sue Riesen, two and one-half miles west of Berne on Indiana Route 218. The Riesens had four daughters, and the oldest, Kathy, had just turned nine. Various relatives showed up for the occasion. Before they left Sue remarked that she had "never seen so many colors of pink, yellow, lilac, and gray" in the sky. "It was beautiful and eerie at the same time," she recalls. The company was gone when the "tornado forecasts," as watches were then called, came across the television. Sue and the four girls went outside and watched the sky from their back steps until Tom told them to come inside, explaining, "We have one chance in a million of getting hit." Sue was not convinced, and she put the girls under a table with candles, water, and some of their toys.

Soon the lights went out. Then Sue "started hearing a noise that got louder and louder." The chance in a million was on its way.

"Get the kids and get in the car," Tom shouted. He planned to go to his father's house in Berne and take shelter in his big basement. It was too late. Outside, the "noise... like many trains" and the sight of "this big, dark gray cloud" containing sticks and leaves let them know they had only seconds to get below ground. The cellar door was outside the house, held in place for winter by a fence staple twisted together. Sue grabbed it and pulled it apart as the family descended to safety. "I always heard of superhuman powers God gives you in life and death situations," Sue says, "and I am now a firm believer. If I hadn't got the door opened we all would have been killed." With Tom's help, Sue held the door shut, fighting the wind that was trying to force it open. "It was as if a monster was trying to get in," Kathy Riesen Vance recalls. She and her sisters were huddled in the corner, Kathy clutching the stuffed orange rabbit she had received as a present only a few hours before. She recalls a "sound like a big explosion and [then] it was silent." Sue's memory is similar. "I heard a loud noise," she says, "and everything was quiet again." Debris blocked the doorway, but the family was able to emerge through a small window. They were afraid to move far, fearful of stepping on live wires or debris. A car finally came down the road. It belonged to neighbors, who took the Riesens to their home. Later that night they made it to Berne and Tom's parents' house.

The Riesen home was destroyed. Only the original 1836 log cabin, around which the rest of the house had been built, the living room, and the kitchen still stood. The roof was gone, but three roofs lay in the front yard, along with clothing, furniture, and all manner of debris. Pieces of their furniture garnished trees across the road. Neighbors who lived a fourth of a mile away, looking out the window after the storm passed, discovered the Riesens' pony in their yard, running around and apparently unhurt after a wild ride. Many neighbors and relatives suffered damage, but it seems unlikely that any had as close a call as this family of six. "The fact that we only had seconds before we would have been killed still haunts me to this day," Kathy says.[8]

Just west of Berne, the tornado "smashed into splinters" a house in which three children were staying alone. Somehow the wind rolled the trio into a carpet before tossing them outside. One suffered head injuries. The other two were unhurt. The town sustained extensive damage to its commercial district along U. S. Route 27. At least ten businesses were severely damaged or destroyed. Two-by-six boards from a nearby lumber yard were found three miles away.[9]

Two views of the Tom and Sue Riesen home. (Kathy Riesen Vance)

A friend at a Berne bowling alley caused concern for nineteen-year old Ken Selking, who lived northwest of Decatur. Selking and another friend had been on a double date at a drive-in theater in New Haven when the screen went dark. At first people honked their horns in protest, then began to file out. The two couples headed to Decatur. "We had no idea what was going on," Selking recalls. "Everything was totally dark," so dark that they were well into Decatur before they even realized they had reached the city. A portable radio finally informed the quartet of the situation. Selking remembered his friend at Berne. He headed south on Route 27 to check on him. It was a hopeless errand. Some five or six miles north of Berne debris blocked the highway. Selking tried county roads, zig-zagging around downed power lines and other debris. Finally those paths, too, were all blocked, and he returned home. He learned the next day that his friend had left Berne before the tornado hit.[10]

Bluffton resident Joe Smekens was four years out of high school and a member of the Indiana National Guard when the tornado hit. He was in his car Palm Sunday evening. The storm, he recalls, shook the vehicle, but he and his passenger thought little of it. He was soon called to Guard duty in Berne, remaining there about a week. As he entered the town on Route 218 he passed a cemetery. All the tombstones were lying flat. It was at that point, Smekens says, that he realized the severity of the storm. The remains of the bowling alley, he remembers, was a popular spot with the Guardsmen. They spent off duty time there bowling, resetting pins by hand and rolling balls back to the bowlers. Another vivid memory is a cement block restaurant with a U-shaped lunch counter. Napkins, salt, pepper, and everything else was in place on the counter just as it had been, but the roof of the restaurant was gone. Another assignment was a chicken farm near town, and Smekens remembers the sight of feathers driven into trees. There were many curiosity seekers, he recalls of the duty, but no looters. It was "a different time," he says, adding, "People in our area were pretty harmless."[11]

East of Berne several witnesses reported seeing two funnels. Larry Lautzenheiser believes them. Lautzenheiser and his wife, Linda, were at home that day on their farm in Blue Creek Township, one mile west of the Ohio border. They had owned the farm for one year. The property included a barn into which his farm machinery would not quite fit. Earlier in the day Larry had told Linda, "I wish that barn would blow away." He had further tempted fate the day before, dropping a one thousand dollar insurance policy on a double corn crib. His refund check came to seven dollars.

Sunday, Lautzenheiser remembers, was a warm day, with temperatures reaching into the low 70s. As evening came, the electricity went off. The couple decided to go to Decatur for some root beer. Linda was carrying their infant son, Stacy, as they headed for the kitchen door. As

Larry opened the door to let her out it slammed shut. Although they did not think of a tornado, Larry recalls, "I knew we were in for something." The couple lay on the living room floor. Dust came up through the carpet, and they could hear objects striking the house. The air pressure "was like going down hill fast," Lautzenheiser notes. "You had to keep swallowing." Then it appeared to be over. The couple stood up, and a second barrage hit. After that all stayed quiet. They went out to discover their car overturned. The barn, corn crib, and other buildings were gone. Only a hog shed and the house remained, but the house was damaged. Although the shingles were all in place, the roof had been lifted and twisted. Newspapers from Kokomo rested near the barn site. Like so many other storm victims, Lautzenheiser remembers numerous anonymous volunteers arriving to help with the clean-up. Many were employees of factories that shut down for lack of power.[12]

Mercer and Van Wert Counties

The tornado's next target was the northwestern edge of Mercer County Ohio. There, along Winkler Road, it would claim two more lives, the first of Ohio's fifty-nine fatalities. Phyllis Wolfe was pronounced dead on arrival at Adams County Memorial Hospital in Decatur, Indiana. Her son Matthew died a few hours later at a hospital in Fort Wayne. Matthew Wolfe was four. Mrs. Wolfe's husband, Robert, and four other children were injured but survived. Linda Tricker, Mrs. Wolfe's sister, lived nearby on Ohio Route 49 with her parents. She visited her sister frequently and had been there the night before the storm. Palm Sunday night she and her future husband went to a movie in Fort Wayne. When they came out they noticed it was very windy, but they did not know anything was wrong until they neared home and encountered roads blocked by debris. Then somebody told them a young woman and little boy had been killed. "I knew right away who it was," Linda recalls. She could think of no other young families in the area. Phyllis, her sister remembers, was always afraid of windstorms. In their attempt to escape this one, her family had gone into a closet, but there was no safe hiding place in the house. It looked, Linda says, like "a big explosion" had occurred.[13]

Elsewhere along Winkler Road the story was the same. One home, the *Rockford Press* reported, "was picked up and torn apart in the air." The couple living there sought shelter in a downstairs coal bin and was not seriously injured. People helping clean up the debris found their personal belongings "strung for miles." Many other homes and barns were damaged or destroyed. Among those damaged was the farm home of Eugene and Rosella Vining. The Vinings were at church with their daughter and son-in-law, Marianna and Ken Fetters, but their sons, Bob and John, were at home. The day, recalls John E. Vining, had been hot "like a blast furnace" and windy. Both John, then ten, and Bob, a college freshman, had begged off attending the service, citing undone homework. Although hitting the books, the boys had the television on. When it and the lights went off, Bob went outside to see what was going on.

John thought he heard a train, thinking little of it until he realized that the nearest railroad was three miles away in the opposite direction of the ever increasing sound. Then Bob burst through the door, threw John to the floor, and covered him with his body. "John, we're in for a big blow," he said, "so keep your head down and your mouth shut." With the house shaking and dust and glass flying, Bob maneuvered John under the piano. Then there was a crash. It was the chimney coming down, bringing walls with it. Silence followed, and the boys realized they had survived. The funnel missed their home by one hundred feet or less.

As their parents returned home from church, they saw flashing lights on the highway and assumed there had been an accident. No, someone explained, "a tornado went right through there," pointing toward their home. When they arrived, Bob reminded his relieved mother of a shed she had wanted him to clean out. "Mom," he announced, "it's clean." So was a barn. The family had a garage with an attached lean-to shed. A car was in each. The lean-to and both cars were unscratched. The garage was never found. One of two hopper wagons in a machine shed was blown away and mangled, the other untouched. Perhaps the strangest sight was a goose blown into a fence post. Its beak had to be pulled out of the post. For the Vinings, the storm produced only one piece of good fortune. A male Brittany spaniel and a female beagle got loose during the storm. The result, John notes, was "probably the finest hunting dog we ever had."[14]

Just two miles south, Duane Hamrick did not even know a tornado had struck. "It looked pretty wicked," he recalls, but more in the manner of a severe storm than a tornado. Hamrick and his wife, Barbara, were visiting at his parents' home when the twister went through. His mother heard on the radio that a tornado had hit Linn Grove, but by the time she got that word, it had passed them. Their first realization of how close they had come was when a Mercer County sheriff's deputy stopped and asked if they had seen anything. Hamrick, familiar with roads leading to the scene, got in the cruiser with him. They had to circle through Indiana to reach the site of the Wolfe family tragedy. A group was prepared to dig through the debris to recover bodies when they were informed that all had been taken to the hospital.[15]

From Mercer County the tornado continued northeast into Van Wert County. "The scene five miles northwest of Rockford on either side of U. S. 33 resembled a battlefield," the *Van Wert Times-Bulletin* reported. "Barns were blown down right and left." The Walnut Grove Methodist

Church, located some eight miles south of Van Wert on U. S. Route 127, was flattened. The weekly Sunday evening youth meeting, which generally took place at the church, had been moved to the parsonage. At Ohio City, officials reacted to the approaching storm with farsighted efficiency. Mayor Vaughn Mottinger called out members of the volunteer fire department, who alerted all the residents. The storm missed the community, but by only a short distance. It leveled a home located a mile and a half south on Route 118, throwing a car from one side of the road into a field on the other side. At least six homes in York Township were damaged or destroyed, as were several farm buildings.[16]

One of the homes belonged to Linus and Irene A. Kill. The Kills and their son, Daniel, were watching Bonanza on television at their Griffen Road home when the lights began to flicker. Irene went to get a flashlight, then started upstairs to secure an oil lamp. While she was out of the room Linus heard reports of tornadoes on television. He did not tell his wife. The Kills had lost a son in a 1948 tornado, and he did not want to upset her. Instead he went to the bathroom to look out the window for threatening weather. As he did, Irene took her first step upstairs. At that instant the windows blew out. "I could just feel that suction," she recalls. She shouted for Linus and Daniel to get to the basement, but her husband did not hear her warning. "There was such a noise in the house," she says, "we couldn't hear anything." As she and Daniel raced for the basement the wind blew a storm door off and "curled it up into a ball." It flew down the steps, barely missing Daniel. The wind caught Irene, blowing her out through the space where the door had been then back inside. "I just flew," she says. She landed, unhurt, in the kitchen against the washer and dryer. Linus had meanwhile started out of the bathroom. He reached for the door just as it blew shut, badly mangling his finger. He joined his family downstairs as another blast went overhead. Possibly it was another twister, or possibly Irene was correct in her opinion that "it was the same one going up and down."

When the Kills finally emerged they discovered that their garage was gone. The car that had been parked inside ended up in a field, some 300 feet away. A two-by-four had crashed through the windshield and exited through the rear window. Just as in 1948, many big trees were down. The entire top story of the house had been twisted, moving six to eight inches out of place. Linus had it removed and rebuilt outward rather than upward. The damage was bad, but one piece of good fortune made it pale to insignificance. The Kills' daughter, Mary Lou, a nursing student, usually stayed home on Sunday evenings, studying on her bed. This night she was working at St. Rita's Hospital in Lima. As the chimney of their home collapsed it hurled bricks all over the unoccupied bed.[17]

For several area residents it was a near miss. "You could tell it was going to do something," recalls Cheryl Freewalt, who lived with her parents on Tomlinson Road in Mercer County, just south of the Van Wert County line. "You just had a feeling." Her parents kept their five children up later than usual just in case. The tornado passed north of them, however. As Carol Place and her fiance rode down Freund Road from her home in Delphos to his parents' house south of Venedocia, nothing about the drive was atypical. After they arrived her fiance's brother-in-law informed them that a tornado had just hit on Freund Road. Not believing him, they returned to take a look, "and there was just devastation all over. We came real close to being in the middle of it," she notes. She did not see the funnel that night. Thirty-seven years later she would, watching as a deadly tornado touched down in Van Wert County in November 2002.[18]

3

"Dad, Outside the Window Is a T..."

Allen and Hancock Counties

"I remember getting there and there was nothing there."

That is how Keaton Vandemark recalls reaching the home of his grandparents, Clair and Elsie Vandemark. Keaton and his parents lived on State Road (which is actually an Allen County road) about three miles south of the village of Gomer. His father was attending a cattle sale in Kentucky, leaving Vandemark and his mother at home alone on Palm Sunday. They were over two miles from the tornado's path, but there was heavy rain and wind strong enough to bend young trees. Then someone appeared at the back door to tell them that a tornado had hit Keaton's grandparents' place. Trees and other debris blocked the way, and the ditches and road ran with water. At a crossroads about one-half mile away from his grandparents' farm, his path was blocked. He walked the rest of the way. Their home, Vandemark says, had been converted from an old school. There was a large barn and seven or eight outbuildings, "and it was all gone."

It took some time for Vandemark to find the home site. Only a hole marked where it had been. The wind had thrown the house nearly 200 yards into a field. Debris from trees was wrapped around it. Vandemark found his grandfather's body, then he heard moaning. It was his grandmother, under the bricks of the chimney. "She was," he remembers, "under what seemed like tons of that stuff." Mrs. Vandemark had several broken bones. She would spend the next two months in the hospital, but, her grandson says, "She was a tough lady." Later she would tell him she "had a sense of flying through the air."[1]

The Vandemarks' daughter, Jane (Vandemark) Miller, lived with her husband, Tom, five miles northwest of Elida. A complicated night of grief began for them about midnight, when Tom's brother, Kenny, arrived with the news. He said he would stay with the couple's children so they could go. Later Tom's parents, Noah and Oletha Miller, ended up with all the kids from both families. Tom's sister-in-law's parents, Ed and Florence Jones, had been hit too. Kenny and his wife, Edith, headed there. The Jones home, it turned out, had been damaged but not destroyed. Florence suffered a broken leg when a cement block from the foundation of their house hit her as she rushed to the basement. They lost a barn and a garage. Their dog, which had been in the garage, returned three days later.

At her parents' place, Jane recalls a scene of "total chaos." Looters had already arrived. The sheriff's department later returned items it had confiscated from some of them. Keaton encountered one looter carrying off his grandfather's Browning shotgun. "I used a little violence," Vandemark told the *Lima News*, "and lifted it from him." Nearby a highway patrolman was using his service revolver to kill badly injured sheep. Soon after Keaton recovered his grandfather's shotgun, the officer cleared everyone from the scene. "He really got forceful, too," Vandemark recalls.

Jane Miller says her mother later told her she thought the television had blown up. She remembered flying through a plate glass window and hitting a clothes line post. "There was not a place on her body she was not black and blue," Jane notes. A piece of debris hit her father in the temple, killing him instantly. He had been in bed when the tornado hit. He was found on his mattress with a sheet covering him. The bed, springs, and other bedding were not found. Mrs. Vandemark kept her grandmother's wedding dress in a box. It was found, intact in the box, nearly three miles away. Mr. Vandemark's car keys, which had been in the ignition of his car, were located two miles away in a tree, his identification still attached. A tire from a combine also rested two miles from the scene. "Everything was absolutely shredded to pieces," Keaton adds. Straw from the barn protruded from trees.[2]

It was close to planting season, and help aplenty arrived. "It was amazing how Mennonites came in and in just a few days completely cleaned the place up," Vandemark recalls. Neighbors formed "chain gangs," Jane Miller says, and walked the fields to pick up all they could. The following Saturday twelve to fifteen neighbors arrived with their tractors and did all the plowing on the eighty-acre farm. Meanwhile, Jane says, the power remained off for several days. She remembers picking out her father's casket by lantern light.[3]

The tornado that killed Mr. Vandemark touched down just west of his farm in Sugar Creek Township. According to the *Lima News*, it moved northeast to State Road, followed it east, then turned northward. It crossed U. S. Highway 30 just west of Cairo, coming frightfully close to that village. Just north of Hook-Waltz Road the storm again turned east, paralleling that road. After again veering northeast, the tornado crossed Interstate 75 just north of Hillville Road. About a mile south of Bluffton the twister entered Hancock County. It lifted just north of Jenera. Along that thirty-five-mile path the F4 twister left thirteen people dead, over one hundred injured, fifty houses and many other buildings largely or totally destroyed, and numerous other homes with damaged roofs and broken windows.[4]

Friends Mike Grove and Mike Roeder of the Gomer area had gone bowling that night with their girlfriends. After dropping off his date, Grove headed south on Gomer Road. Nearing an intersection a flash of lightning illuminated a "weird yellow sky." Then he spotted the funnel to his south. Cattle were running across a field toward a barn. When the next bolt of lightning flashed, they were gone. Grove assumed they had made it to the barn. He later learned that they had not. The funnel lifted briefly, sparing a home located at the intersection. Then it came down again, and Grove saw sparks from power lines in its path. He looked southeast as the Vandemark home "just disappeared." He drove to the site, noting, "It was one of the worst things I've ever seen. I didn't go any further when I saw what it did to their place," he says.

"I'll never forget that day," Mike Roeder asserts. After bowling, he and his girlfriend stopped at an ice cream stand, where they learned that there were tornado warnings out. Going down Cable Road it was very dark. "You could sense something," he says. "It was eerie." Grayish-green "puffball" clouds dotted the sky. Then, against the twilight, "I saw this funnel [that] looked like a little snake." It was three or four miles away, and Roeder tried to get away by heading perpendicular to its path. At State Road big trees around them were falling. Either the tornado had caught them or, more likely in Roeder's opinion, a second one had developed. He turned east on State Road. "All of a sudden," he says, "there was a big flash." The tornado had hit high tension derricks, tearing them "right down to the ground." A repairman later told him that only in Texas had he seen towers taken down so close.[5]

On the west side of Cairo, Ruth Hurley called her husband, Richard, and her children into the house. It had been a breezy evening recalls one of those children, Larry Hurley. He is not sure why his mother summoned everybody inside, but it was a prescient move. The breeze suddenly stopped, the birds quit singing, and the sky grew darker. Richard went outside to have a look as the wind picked up again. To the southwest he saw sparks from falling power lines. The family watched as the funnel appeared, lifting and touching down again. It headed into a woods, flinging treetops into the air. Richard ordered his family into the basement. He looked out a cellar window and saw the funnel heading directly toward Cairo. Mr. Hurley watched as it lifted a roof from a house west of the village cemetery and lowered it back down in place. Then the twister veered north, sparing the village.[6]

North of Cairo, two fathers began frantic searches in the wake of the storm. One ended happily, the *Lima News* reported. The other did not. Homer Smith had come home from work at about 6:30. He heard the storm warnings on television, "but I figured it was north of us," he later explained. The TV reception was poor that night, and Smith and his wife, June, decided to forego watching Bonanza and go to bed. He went to the kitchen to turn off the lights. "Then," he told *News* reporter Hope Strong, "I heard a roar like a train locomotive." The power went off, "and I felt like I was being lifted... the house too. I was in a tunnel," Smith continued, "trying to grab at something, but couldn't." His next memory was rolling over and over through a field.

The twister destroyed this barn in Allen County. (Mike Roeder)

Little remained of the Clair Vandemark home on State Road. (Mike Grove)

The Night of the Wicked Winds 31

Remains of homes near Cairo (above) and near Gomer (below). (Mike Grove)

Getting up Smith's thoughts immediately turned to his wife and three daughters. He went to a neighbor's home for assistance in his search, then headed for his car, where he had a flashlight. Smith quickly found one daughter. Then he heard a woman screaming. "I presumed it was my wife," Smith said of the woman, who was pinned under a tree. As he headed toward her he encountered a stranger, who turned out to be the woman's husband. "He asked me if I had found any kids," Smith said. Smith told the man he had not, then asked if the stranger had seen any little girls. The man, dazed and confused, muttered something that led Smith to realize that he had not. He reached the woman, and with the help of a motorist he flagged down, got her out from under the tree. Smith's wife and other two daughters were eventually found. Mrs. Smith and one of the children were seriously injured. The other two girls suffered only minor injuries. The story had a much sadder ending for the stranger. His two children, one two years and the other five months old, drowned when the car in which the family was riding was thrown into a creek. His wife died Monday morning at a Lima hospital.[7]

David and Margaret Rusmisel, who lived on a farm south of Beaverdam, spent Sunday afternoon and evening at the funeral home. Margaret's father had died Friday night. As they returned home, Margaret later wrote, "The car was buffeted by wind. Utility wires danced. Branches blew." They arrived home to a dark house, the power out, but as they looked for candles the lights came back on. So did the radio. It told of a tornado to the northwest in the vicinity of David's parents' home. Paul and Verna Rusmisel had been caring for Laura, David and Margaret's youngest daughter. David tried to call, but could only get an incessant busy signal. A neighbor on the party line picked up and announced, "There's been a tornado in their area."

With that David, Margaret, and their other children rushed to their car and headed north into the darkness. Paul and Verna lived on Slabtown Road in Monroe Township. As they got close a deputy stopped them and said they could go no further. "We have family there," the Rusmisels explained, and the deputy waved them on with a warning to be alert for downed power lines. "Suddenly," Margaret later recorded, "we're in a no-man's land. Dirt. Trees. Stumps. Limbs. Fence. Nothing familiar." Eventually they reached and hesitantly identified the pile of rubble that had been the Rusmisel home. The wind had picked it up, twisted it, carried it across the driveway, and, Margaret says, "put it down in a heap." The nearby barn was "just kindling."

Two people at the scene said they had helped load Paul, Verna, and Laura into an ambulance bound for Lima Memorial Hospital. With that information, the Rusmisels drove to Lima. They reached a hospital crowded with injured people and the staff and volunteers who had arrived to offer assistance. With the help of a nurse they found Laura in a crib and Paul in a chair by her side. Laura, who had been in her grandmother's arms, was only scratched. Paul had black eyes, straw in his hair, and only one shoe. Verna was in surgery. A sill from the house had landed across her abdomen, leaving her with a crushed pelvis. The good news was that the blood covering her legs had turned out to be red paint. Still, she was facing over two months in the hospital. She would later relate that she had looked through a door and seen her assailant, "something big and black and green that was bouncing."[8]

Beyond Cairo one resident of Hook-Waltz Road lost two houses and five barns. His 1965 car was a piece of "flattened steel out in the field." In the aftermath of the storm he recovered the body of a neighbor woman. She had been blown three hundred feet beyond her house. A short distance east, northwest of Beaverdam, the storm destroyed two more homes. In one of them the young family rushed for the basement, but it was too late. "By then," a family member told the *News*, "the wind was whipping us through the dining room." She and her husband dropped to the floor, shielding their children beneath them. All survived, but the top floor of their house was gone and sections of walls below were missing. Their deep freezer landed a mile away.[9]

At Beaverdam a new pastor had just arrived at the Church of Christ. There was a practice scheduled that night for the Easter sunrise service that the church always conducted with the Methodist Church. The pastor, wanting to get to know his new parishioners, had insisted on holding a fellowship service after the practice. His decision produced some grumbling, but as things turned out, it was an inspired move. Among those there were Rex Ferrall, his wife, Nettie, and four of their children. During the service someone came in and said a tornado had struck near Van Wert. Ferrall decided to return to his home on Hillville Road. The storm had hit by then, and utility poles and other debris marked much of his route home. He passed destroyed homes as well, stopping at one to assist a lady who had been injured. His own home had roof damage. The foundation had been moved, but the house was livable. Ferrall's daughter Vickie was home when the tornado struck. Heeding instructions she had learned that week at school, she went to the basement upon hearing the approaching storm. Nettie was a part time nurse at the Bluffton Hospital. She was called in for a very busy work night.[10]

Also attending the service were Doyt and Wilda Hanthorn, along with daughters Sandra, Mary, and Susan. They stayed at the church when word of the tornado arrived, leaving about 9:30 for their home a mile and a half north of the village on Route 696. As they got closer, Wilda says, "It was just a mess." Then one of the girls asked, "Where's our house?" They looked, and, "There was nothing there. It picked it up off the foundation," Wilda explains, "and blew it up." Doyt, a World War II veteran and prisoner of war, recalls, "I've never seen anything like it." About all the family would salvage were a saucer, a cup, and a few coins. Later someone who lived near Lake Erie mailed back

Wilda's high school diploma. Susan's cat limped home, its back legs broken, then died. The Hanthorns had only the clothes on their backs, not even a comb or a toothbrush.

Neighbors Willis and Wanda Boutwell took in the family. Later they moved into the home of a woman whose husband had died a few weeks earlier. Fearful of living alone, she had moved in with a sister. From this base, the family began the process of rebuilding their lives. "The first thing we went to buy," Wilda notes, "was a Bible." Help came in many forms. Carloads of youngsters arrived to help with the clean-up. The Beaverdam town hall became a clearinghouse. Meals were available there, as well as clothing and household items. Wilda remembers receiving cards with money in them and going to pay for items she had purchased only to discover that persons unknown had already paid the bill.[11]

The Hanthorns' neighbors, Fred and Pat Arnold, were also present at the Beaverdam service, along with their children, Mark and Ann. They decided to go home when they heard about the tornado. "We never made it," Fred notes. A short distance south of his parents' home Fred stopped, left his family in the car, and walked to his folks' place. "I got there," he says, "and there was nothing standing." He found both of his parents close to where their home had been. His mother, Velma, was obviously "in bad shape." His father, Merrill, had a horrible gash in the back of his head and was incoherent. Arnold went back and got his car. His father was able to walk to the car. Ed Sutter of the Beaverdam Fire Department, who had come on his own to see if anyone needed aid, helped him carry his mother to the car. Arnold took both of his parents to the Bluffton Hospital. His mother died a few hours later. Mr. Arnold remained in the hospital for a week but recovered from his wound.

The basement was all that remained of Merrill Arnold's two-story frame home. Two barns, three sheds, and two garages were also gone, but a car in one of the garages was unmoved. None of their appliances were ever found. A one-pound coffee can was stuck most of the way into a tree but was not bent. Mr. Arnold later told his son that all he could remember was making it to the landing on his way to the basement.

Fred Arnold's home, which he rented, was totaled as well. The family salvaged only a few items. Like the Hanthorns, Arnold says the outpouring of help was impressive. Among those providing assistance was a Jewish youth group composed of high school and college age individuals. They stayed in dorms at Bluffton College and helped rebuild a number of homes and barns. Their willingness to perform any work, no matter how menial, impressed Arnold. After one of the barn raisings, he recalls, the local folk hosted a square dance for the kids. They enjoyed it so much that a second was later held. Locally, Walt Beck, the Beaverdam fire chief, arranged for surplus tools, clothing, and many other needed items. He also coordinated much of the clean-up. Bill Begg donated a beef, which was ground into hamburger to keep the volunteers fed. A Red Cross official, Arnold remembers, arrived and told Beck and Begg that they would have to charge people for the hamburgers because the Red Cross was charging for things they gave people. One of the two replied by telling the official "to go back to Lima and stay there." Despite that one incident, the recovery effort, Arnold notes, "really brought Richland Township together."[12]

Three miles northwest of Beaverdam, Virgil and Vera Allgire rode out a strong thunderstorm with their children, Mike and Susan. When it passed they started to bed. Then Mike saw the flashing lights of emergency vehicles. The family went to investigate, but officials turned them back at the junction of Cool and Hillville Roads. The next morning Virgil and Mike joined a search party that covered the four miles between Route 696 and Bentley Road. Some people were still reported as missing, but they turned out to be alive and well. They had been unable to reach family members because of communications being down.

School was canceled for the next few days, Mike recalls, and he joined fellow student volunteers in the relief effort. Officials divided the youths into crews and took them to different farms. There they gathered, stacked, and burned debris. Many of the sights are still deeply etched in his mind. At one farm a hay baler sat upside down in the basement of a destroyed home. At another his group discovered an eight-foot tall transformer which had blown about one-quarter of a mile and crashed through a brick house, killing the woman who lived there. Walking through a wooded section near Hillville and Phillips Roads, it took twenty minutes to get through one hundred yards of woods. "My feet hardly ever touched the ground," Allgire recalls. The floor frame of a mobile home that had disappeared about one mile west of Cairo was found northeast of Beaverdam, some seven miles away. East of Interstate 75, Allgire listened as an insurance man talked to a farmer whose barn had collapsed on top of a herd of beef cattle. The farmer was incredulous as the insurance man insisted that the hopelessly trapped cattle would not be covered if he shot them to end their suffering. As Allgire walked away he heard the shots.[13]

It was a normal day, a pretty day, says Joyce (Reichenbach) Beery, who lived on a forty-acre farm near Hillville and Swaney Roads. Her grandmother, Eva Clymer, had come from Findlay that day. She planned to stay a week. As night came down Mrs. Clymer was in the living room watching Bonanza. Watching with her were Joyce's father, Ulysses Reichenbach; her stepmother, Betty; and her stepbrother, Jim Steiner. Another stepbrother, Joe Steiner, was upstairs in bed. A third, John Steiner, was also upstairs, helping Joyce with her algebra homework. Joyce's brother, Richard Reichenbach, was away on a church date.

It began to rain, Joyce recalls, then it grew harder. She got up to close a hallway window. As she did, "the window blew out and the floor tilted." She ran into John's room, and both jumped under his bed. "That," Joyce says, "was the last we remembered."

She awoke in a neighbor's corn field. To get there she had blown over her family's orchard, landing at least one hundred yards away. "It was very black and very wet," and Joyce had a cut heal, and a stick was protruding from her right arm, and she had absolutely no idea how she had ended up in this field. John and Joyce had held onto each other as they dived under the bed, and they landed not far apart. He got up first, virtually uninjured, and was calling for his stepsister. They found each other then heard Mr. Reichenbach shouting. He was in the debris that had been his house, his ribs badly fractured. He found Betty. She was much more seriously hurt. A group lifted her into a neighbor's station wagon for the trip to the hospital. Joe was found dead. So was Mrs. Clymer. The neighbor took Mr. and Mrs. Reichenbach to the Lima Hospital. There Betty died during surgery.

Joyce's brother, who was deaf, came home from his date to this frightful scene. The frame house was leveled. They salvaged Mr. Reichenbach's Air Force scrapbook, some of Joyce's grandmother's quilts, a few pictures, a few slides, and nothing else. The barn was also destroyed. All of the animals except the family dog were killed.

Three sets of aunts and uncles took in the children and, until he fully recuperated, Mr. Reichenbach. He eventually moved into another home he owned, which he had been renting. Joyce's stepsister, Sally, who lived in Columbus, handled the funeral arrangements. Neither Joyce nor her father was able to attend.[14]

On Palm Sunday afternoon, Janice Arnold and Charles W. Amstutz were married at the Beaverdam Methodist Church. "It was a very warm and windy day," Janice recalls. After the wedding the couple drove to Dayton for the start of a one-week honeymoon with no fixed itinerary. They returned to Allen County that Thursday, a bit earlier than they had planned. They had not read a newspaper or listened to a news broadcast, and, Janice notes, "We knew absolutely nothing about what had happened." Their first clue came when they reached Bluffton, Charles's hometown, and noticed that they could not see Arthur and Edith Swank's horse barn. The Swanks had raised Amstutz's father after his mother died, becoming surrogate grandparents to Charles. After observing the damage to the Swank property, the couple saw a swath of downed trees. Amstutz's father, Wilbur, was mayor of Bluffton. Charles and Janice went to city hall, where the chief of police informed them of what had happened. They also learned of the death of Janice's aunt, Velma Arnold.

The Swank home had been destroyed. Arthur and Edith had changed into their night clothes just before the tornado hit. Mr. Swank went to close a breezeway door when he heard a sound "like twelve freight trains coming across the field." They dashed to the basement. The moment they reached it the house was gone. A water heater fell on Mrs. Swank, breaking her leg. "She was never herself after," Charles says. Several of their horses were killed.[15]

On Phillips Road, near old U. S. Route 25 (soon to be replaced by I-75), Carol (Steiner) Bell was babysitting Cindy and Mindy Quellhorst. The girls' parents, Ralph and Sue Quellhorst, had picked Carol up at the home of her parents, Evan and Betty Steiner, then gone to a young couples' meeting in Bluffton. Quellhorst was the pastor at the United Church of Christ on Phillips Road. The parsonage, where Carol was taking care of the girls, was located diagonally across the road. As they headed for Bluffton, Sue told her husband that she had heard storm warnings. "Look at the sky," he replied. At the time it was perfectly clear. That quickly changed. After watching hail during the meeting, the Quellhorsts decided to return home. They had no idea what their babysitter had just experienced.

Carol stayed with the two-and-a-half-year old twins frequently. After putting the girls to bed she heard the tornado forecasts on television. Tornadoes had hit the Bluffton area before, and she listened carefully but was not yet overly concerned. Meanwhile she put her hair in rollers, worked on a term paper for school, and received a brief visit from her boyfriend and future husband, Tom Bell. As it began to storm harder, she began to consider taking the girls to the basement. Her father soon called and urged her to do so. Rev. Quellhorst had a downstairs study, and all three sat in a large chair there. "They were confused," Carol says of the girls, "but they went along with whatever I did." When the lights went out, she adds, "I just started to talk to them because I was scared too." Before long she heard the freight train sound, "that typical sound." The basement windows blew out, and Carol says, "I could start to feel this tremendous pressure." More frightening was a feeling of suction, as if she was being pulled from above. Then, "there was crashing and rain." Things fell down around them, and thoughts raced through Carol's mind: "Are we going to die? What about my mom and dad? What about my grandma?"

As things grew quiet, she began singing to the girls. "It made me feel better," she recalls, "and they were relaxed." Carol tried to find something to cover them all and keep the heavy rain off. It was dark by then, and she worried who would ever find them. Through it all the girls were troopers. "They didn't complain about being wet," Carol notes, "they didn't cry." She and the girls remained there an hour or more. Then Carol thought she heard someone call her name. It was her father and her brother, Greg. "They were very frightened," she says. They had come on foot, passing destruction all along the way, culminating with the sight of the demolished parsonage. The two made their way into the basement, and Carol and the girls climbed over a freezer and other things to get out. A nearby motorist took them to the United Church of Christ parsonage in Bluffton.

Meanwhile the Quellhorsts had tried to reach home via three routes, all blocked by debris. On the third attempt they saw a man and his wife in their pajamas walking across a field. They had been asleep when the tornado destroyed their house and threw them from a second-story bedroom into a field. The couple was cut and bruised. Ralph and Sue took them to the Bluffton Hospital, then accompanied by Bluffton's Lutheran pastor, a good friend, Ralph tried again to get home. He left Sue, pregnant with the couple's third child, behind. They got close enough to see that the parsonage was gone. "I guess I got a little crazy," Rev. Quellhorst admits. People at the scene restrained him from charging through downed power lines. Soon Evan Steiner appeared to reassure him. They returned again to Bluffton and the family was reunited. The pastor then went to the Bluffton Hospital to check on parishioners. This created fear and confusion for Sue's parents when they arrived from Upper Sandusky and were told that Ralph had been seen at the hospital.

About dawn the next morning, Rev. Quellhorst returned home. He went to the church, where the sanctuary had been blown apart. As the sun came up he heard the sounds of tractors and trucks. It was volunteers, ready to begin the job of cleaning up. Later, in response to an anonymous telephone call, he met a man at a local restaurant. The stranger explained that God had spared his daughter, keeping her safe as she traveled along I-75 when the tornado hit. He gave the pastor a $2,500 check for the rebuilding process. Equally important to Rev. Quellhorst was the nickel he received from a friend in the Philippines. The friend got it from a school girl whom he had informed of the storm.

The Quellhorsts moved into the new parsonage in September. The new church building opened in August 1966. Meanwhile the pastor was helping plan for future disasters. He established an insurance plan for United Churches of Christ. He also organized a disaster response program. It started in Ohio and West Virginia. Today it has grown into a national program with several thousand people involved. He explains, "People need to be organized if you're going to help."

Carol Bell came through her ordeal with only scratches on her legs. The girls were untouched. With much justification, the *Lima News* proclaimed her "one of the night's unsung heroines." She, however, gives much of the credit to her father. "Dad called at the perfect time," she says, explaining that she might have delayed going after the girls otherwise. Whoever is deserving of the credit, she concludes, "It was indeed a miracle."[16]

Entering Hancock County, the tornado charged eastward along State Route 103 before veering a bit northward. Two and one-half miles east of Bluffton it blew a house along the highway to pieces, killing its two occupants. Nearby, Leona B. Sheldon of Findlay was driving home from Washington, D. C., where she and her colleagues from a Bluffton glove factory had attended the Cherry Blossom Festival. Approaching the intersection of Routes 103 and 235, she looked south, as she later told her daughter, Barbara L. Smith, "and there was a wall of water coming at her." It rocked the car but passed over quickly. In its wake she could see downed trees and damaged homes. Stopping to catch her breath a short way down the road, she noticed power lines down as well. A police officer pulled up and informed the ladies that they should not be there. A tornado had struck the area, the dutiful patrolman explained. To that the shaken lady explained that she had not had any choice in the matter.[17]

Just three-tenths of a mile north along Route 235, Robert K. "Bob" Flick also had no say concerning the tornado. His sister and brother-in-law had been visiting on what he remembers as a "real warm, balmy day." They left just ten or fifteen minutes before the storm hit. Flick's sons, Thomas L. and Mark A., were in bed, as was his daughter, Mary Kathleen. His wife, Mary E., was watching Bonanza. The station broke in with a warning of possible tornadoes and the useless advice to open east windows. Mary came into the bathroom, where Flick was, and opened the window in there. She then headed upstairs to get the kids. As she started up, Mary Kathleen was descending. "Dad," she said, "outside the window is a t..." With that, Flick says, "everything blew up." Something, possibly a door frame, struck him in the head, then the house exploded, "just opened up."

Flick and his daughter were thrown about ten feet. She became caught in debris, but got up and ran toward him. An "indistinct glow" allowed Bob to see. "Out of the sky," he says, "was coming big hunks of something." He yelled for Mary Kathleen to get down, and she dived under him. When they could get up safely, they went to one of their cars. Flick thought it would be warm inside, but all the glass had been blown out. Mud and soybean stalks were all over the driver's side. He managed to get it started, began to back up, then realized that his wife or sons might be behind. He shined the lights toward the house, except there was no house there. "All my mind could think of," he recalls, "was the piano lying on somebody." Flick and Mary Kathleen yelled out for anybody, and Mrs. Flick shouted back, "I have the boys." They had been blown east-northeast about fifteen rods. Mary, starting up the stairs, was pushed down and ended up sitting on a toy box. Tom was worried about his dog. They found him, unhurt but covered with fuel oil from an overturned tank.

The Flicks got in the car and started for the Bluffton Hospital. They got only a short distance before debris blocked their way. As Flick turned around in a driveway he saw a man standing on the debris of his house. "All he could say," Flick recalls, "was, 'If I could find my shoes I think I could find them.'" He repeated it over and over. "Them" turned out to be the man's in-laws, both of whom were killed.

They finally reached the hospital. "It was full of people," Flick says. With many life-threatening cases to deal with, hospital employees instructed the Flicks to wait. Both Bob and Mark required stitches to the head. "I don't know where I landed," Mark told his father, "but it seemed soft." As for Mary Kathleen, "Debris had just filled her skin." Nurses placed her in a tub to get the worst of it out, but it took months for it all to fester and work its way out. Although their house was gone, the Flicks were well. As for possessions, they recovered three: a damaged refrigerator, a toaster without a handle that remains in use, and a Bible, opened to a page in the Book of Isaiah telling about a whirlwind.[18]

Seneca County

The Allen and Hancock County tornado touched down at about 9:30. About forty-five minutes later another F4 hit south of Alvada in Seneca County. It may have been the same twister descending again, as its location suggested, or it may have been a separate funnel. Either way the result was more death and destruction. An electric transmission tower was the storm's first target. North of Carey in Big Spring Township the tornado did over $100,000 in damage at the Smith-Douglas Division factory of the Borden Company. According to the *Tiffin Advertiser-Tribune*, the main building at the facility, a 100-by-100-foot concrete structure, "practically collapsed." The manager, who lived in a house trailer at the site, fled in his car when he heard warnings placing the plant in the storm's path. Moving a little north of east through the county, the twister smashed barns, removed roofs, and blew down trees. In Eden Township, just east of State Route 100, the wind brought down a large barn, trapping twenty-six dairy cattle and sixty pigs. Humane Society Agent Gaylord Webb directed the effort of neighboring farmers to rescue as many of the animals as possible. The group was able to save seventeen cattle and fifty-seven of the pigs.[19]

The tornado struck savagely at a tiny community on U. S. Highway 224 and State Route 67. "The hamlet of Rockaway," the *Republic Reporter* announced, "is no more." Only three homes were left standing there. Among the homes destroyed was that of Francis and Theresa Leibengood and their children, Dan, Alan, and Mary. It was a large farm house, two and one-half stories, recalls Dan Leibengood. One of Leibengood's uncles had died, and the family returned late that evening from the funeral home. Soon it was storming. As his mother put Mary to bed, Dan was watching the lightning from his bedroom window. He watched as the wind blew down a large pine tree in the yard. By then, "The wind was roaring," and Dan realized this might be a tornado. He ran to his brother's room and alerted him, then kept running to get downstairs. Reaching for a door knob was his last memory in the house.

"The next thing I knew," Leibengood says, "I was flat on my face buried in bricks." Their weight made it nearly impossible for him to breathe. He heard his father call for his mother, then heard family members searching for him. For some reason he could not respond for a time. Finally he yelled, "Hey, I'm over here." Unfortunately all his mother could see of "over here" was a three-foot pile of bricks, and she started screaming. Francis asked his son where he was, to which Dan replied, "You're standing on me." His father dug him out, and he eventually reached Mercy Hospital in Tiffin, where he received a tetanus shot. "It was packed," Leibengood says of the local hospital. The roof and the north wall of their house were gone. Theresa had covered Mary with her body as the tornado struck. She looked up to see the lights of cars passing on Route 224. In addition to their home, the family lost a large barn and other outbuildings.[20]

Two Rockaway residents were killed. One was a woman who was struck in the head by a brick after she had reached her basement. Her husband and her mother were seriously injured. The other was Donald Egbert, who died of his injuries twenty-nine days later. His son, Larry T. Egbert, recalls that it all started with a thunderstorm. Mr. Egbert and his wife, Catherine, had been visiting relatives that day. When they returned Larry was watching television upstairs. His mother began to iron a dress to wear to work the next day. When the lights went out she at first thought the iron had blown a fuse. Then she realized it was the storm. She told her husband to put all his money in his wallet, then went upstairs to get Larry. The three started for the basement, but no one made it. They saw a glass porch blow away, "and in a split second," Larry recalls, "we were down." Donald Egbert later said he "went on an airplane ride through the whole house." He was thrown outside, rolled up in a rug. His wife was under a deep freeze. Larry was covered with bricks. His hands and his feet were touching his shoulders, and he could only move his fingers.

A passing motorist, Lorin Knierieman, arrived to help. He found Mr. Egbert first. Then he attempted to wrest the freezer off Catherine, but it was filled with meat and he could not budge it. Mrs. Egbert urged him instead to look for Larry. He did, walking on the bricks until Larry shouted, "You're putting pressure on my head." With the assistance of others who showed up to help, Knierieman dug him out. Larry and his father rode in the same ambulance to Mercy Hospital. Larry was covered with soot, and as he entered the hospital a nurse exclaimed, "Oh my God! It hit the colored district!" Larry would recover, but his injuries would linger for the rest of his life.

42   *The Night of the Wicked Winds*

Remains of the Donald Egbert home. (Donna Fox, Larry Egbert)

Bricks under which Larry Egbert was buried. (Fox/Egbert)

The Night of the Wicked Winds 43

The Egbert family automobile after the tornado. (Fox/Egbert)

Bridge damage on State Route 67, Seneca County. (Fox/Egbert)

His sister, Donna K. (Egbert) Fox, was at a dance in Bascom that night. Before leaving she had joked to her father, "I'll see you later if a tornado doesn't take you." She had no idea of the irony of her comment until her future father-in-law came to the dance to get her and her boyfriend. He took Donna to her aunt's home in Republic. Her grandparents picked her up there and took her to the hospital. With difficulty she located her father, but, "I didn't even know him," she says. She also visited her mother and brother. About daylight her grandfather took her home. He tried to prepare her for what she was about to see. Despite his effort, "When I got there, I couldn't believe it." She walked around, still wearing the formal dress she would have on for the next four days. Donna remembers a looter walking off with pictures. "She won't need them," the thief told police, "she's dead." Several lawn mowers from her father's business also disappeared. Her fourteen-room home was a pile of debris. Donna and Larry found no sign of the new bedroom furniture they had gotten the day before. One key was found from the family's new piano. A check was found in Huntsburg, Pennsylvania.

Donna tried to return for the remainder of her senior year of high school. She was frequently summoned to the hospital because of her father's deteriorating condition. School officials finally told her to stay home. They allowed her to be graduated. Her mother, still in a wheelchair, also attended the ceremony.[21]

Further east, on Route 224, Herval Thallman escaped disaster by about 800 feet. Thallman and his wife, Claudine, heard radio reports of a tornado near Van Wert. Thallman assumed it would "get blown out" long before it reached his farm. That storm had, but Seneca County's twister was approaching his place at F4 intensity. It hit his barn, collapsing the one hundred-by-forty-five-foot structure, on top of a herd of fifty-three Angus cattle. Thirty were killed. The next morning the Clinton Township Volunteer Fire Department helped get the others out. His house, those 800 feet away, escaped damage.[22]

About three-fourths of a mile northeast of the junction of U. S. 224 and State Route 19, Wayne and Mildred Biller were home with their son, Jim. Members of their citizens' band radio club dropped by, and the group followed the paths of various storms through CB reports. It was not long after the club members left that a heavy electrical storm hit. Then, through the lightning, Wayne saw the funnel, shouting, "There it is!" Following the next flash-- Mildred wanted to see it, too-- the family headed for the basement. They crawled in a potato bin behind the basement steps. They did not hear anything, but felt a tremendous pressure in their ears. Mildred was lifted a slight distance off the floor, but a chimney fell on the bin and held it in place. The bin, in turn, held the Billers.

After the storm passed the Billers crawled from the debris of their home, which they had extensively remodeled the previous year. It had been destroyed, as had a large barn and a chicken coop. Sheep had been killed, and chickens, plucked by the wind, "were running around with no feathers." About all that remained was a fourteen-inch statue of Mother Mary. It was outside surrounded by a half buried bathtub. The tub was destroyed, but the statue was only scratched.

Wayne guided his family through downed power lines. Then he retrieved neighbor Rosella Joiner, who was shouting from a field. "She was just peppered," Mildred remembers, with stones and other pieces of debris. Wayne and Bob Depinet, a neighbor, put her in a station wagon and took her to Wayne's parents' home. Mrs. Joiner's brick home had been destroyed. Rescuers found her husband, George, under a door and other debris. The Joiners and George's mother, who lived with the couple, had been in bed when the storm hit. They ended up in their basement. All were injured, but they survived.[23]

Wayne Biller (right) surveys the remains of his home. (Mildred Biller)

4
Toledo's Tornado

Lucas County

It started in the vicinity of Sylvania Avenue and Woodley Road at about 9:30 p.m., continued east then northeast through both residential and commercial neighborhoods, and ended somewhere in Lake Erie. When it was over, Toledo's tornado had left eighteen people dead, over 230 injured, and devastated the northern edge of Ohio's fourth largest city. It was considered, The *Toledo Blade* reported, "the worst natural disaster in the city's history."

As the storm headed east from the touchdown point, it blew out windows and flattened the roofs of businesses. At Sylvania and Secor two men were on their way to get hamburgers when the storm hit. They were blown backward into the parking lot of the drive in. "I don't know what hit me," one said, "except I woke up on the parking lot and my head and arm were bleeding." Both men were treated for cuts, as were seventeen people in the drive in. The roof of the business was gone. Continuing east the storm also blew the roof off a department store at Sylvania and Douglas Road and damaged several homes in the area. The E. I. du Pont de Nermours & Co. paint factory at the junction of Tremainsville Road and Upton Avenue sustained a loss of over $150,000. Three buildings were wrecked, and a 150-foot smokestack was toppled. More stores lost roofs as the storm veered northeast. On Laskey Road the winds ripped a portion of the roof from the Glass Bowl Lanes.[1]

During this early stage of the storm, Ken Rutkowski was returning to his home at 4726 Monroe Street. He had been visiting a friend who lived three miles south. Returning home he came up Secor Road instead of his usual route on Tallmadge, hoping to avoid the storm. He had no idea it was a tornado. All he observed were heavy rains and wind. He arrived at home to discover a huge oak tree across his driveway. His wife, Virginia, had ridden out the storm, running upstairs and getting in bed with their daughter, Janet. She may have heard a roaring noise, she says, but sharp lightning provided the more vivid memory. Although their home was not seriously damaged, a cement block building about fifty feet from their driveway, which was part of a nursery, was knocked down.[2]

Another early victim of the tornado was the Bettinger Farms and Greenhouse, Inc., located at the corner of Secor Road and Sylvania Avenue. Brothers Harold and Leonard Bettinger owned the three-acre facility, which they had purchased in 1964 to expand their business. Harold's son, William, operated it. The day before, William had told the staff there would not be any work for a time; the crop had to be grown. Those staff members would be called back much sooner than he expected.

William and his wife, Suzanne, took advantage of the warm Sunday, taking a portable television outside to watch a movie. Toward evening it grew dark and cool, then "extremely calm." The birds quit singing, and Bettinger remembers thinking, "Something's not right." They went inside and it started to rain. The rain and the wind soon got hard. William wanted to go out and start the greenhouse circulating pumps, but Suzanne told him to wait until after the storm. It was good advice. Bettinger heard a "horrifically loud rushing sound," so loud that he could not hear the many panes of glass breaking over the roar. But they were breaking. The funnel did not touch down, but it removed a wood water tower, sending its planks through the roof of the office building.

At 4:00 a.m., Bettinger and members of the staff went out to try to salvage as many plants as possible. Pieces of glass were still falling-- and would continue to fall for over a week-- so he secured hard hats and leather gloves. They removed glass particles from the crop. Other greenhouses offered their facilities to store the plants, an invaluable gesture with three nights of freezes ahead. Several dump truck loads of glass ended up in a nearby landfill. The flying glass had stripped the paint off the west side of cars parked nearby. A maple tree in the Bettingers' yard sparkled from the glass for over a year. Eventually miles of two-inch pipe had to be replaced. Damage to the facility totaled about seventy-five percent. It was two years before it was fully operational. Adding to the difficulties were sightseers, still in their Easter clothes, who arrived the next Sunday. Some thought a devastated greenhouse would make an interesting tourist site. Others were simply stealing plants. "Things were still breaking," Bettinger recalls, and he was forced to run them off "without any politeness" for their own safety.[3]

To the east, the tiny community of Alexis, east of Stickney Avenue and north of Matzinger Road, was hard hit. At least two homes were destroyed on Tralger Drive, and several garages were flattened or unroofed. At 865 Tralger Drive the Edward Extine family was watching Bonanza on television. Storm warnings occasionally appeared. Edward noticed wind and lightning and sent son John out to his truck to get a large flashlight. Edward returned and reported that his older brother's car was "tipping." Then he shouted, "Here it comes!" as the front door blew open. Another son, Jerry, was standing by the picture window. The wind crashed through it, depositing Jerry in a hallway. The family of six converged in the three boys' bedroom because it seemed the safest place in the home, which had no basement. From there they looked up and saw stars twinkling in the suddenly calm night.

Jerry's ride to the hospital was "pretty scary" he recalls, with power lines down all along the route. He would wash his hair "for days," trying to get out embedded dirt, sand, and tiny pieces of debris. Other members of the family required stitches but were not seriously hurt. Their house was. The entire roof was gone, and most of their furniture was lost. Their 1963 Ford was atop a pickup truck. A flatbed truck that Edward used in his lumber hauling business was blown between 200 and 300 yards and destroyed. Their neighbors' house remained at its same location, but exactly upside down. Another home had a telephone pole lodged in it. Through it all there was one fragile survivor. Jerry's sister, Joyce (Extine) Ruch, found a Beatles record amidst the debris of their home. A picture of her holding the album made the front page of the *Toledo Blade*. Capital Records learned of it and sent her a box of records.[4]

Nearby Raceway Park was also hit. Myron Jones was running a horse, Aclarando, there at the time. As he returned to his home at Bowling Green that Sunday afternoon he noticed a large black cloud behind him. "It looked very ferocious," he recalls, "and it appeared to be heading northeast. I remember a short tail sticking down... as it proceeded." Barn Seven, Aclarando's home, was not hit. Other parts of the track were. Jones went there the next day, and "things were really in a mess." So was the Toledo Scale Company, located across the street.[5]

From Alexis the twister crossed Interstate 75. In its path was a northbound car. Both the driver and his passenger were pipefitters heading for a job in Detroit. The passenger was killed, but the driver had only minor injuries. He told reporters that the vehicle landed on a parallel road after it stopped rolling. Two tractor-trailers bound for Indianapolis, driven by friends, were also overturned on the expressway. Both drivers were briefly hospitalized for minor injuries. "It's like a miracle," one of them told the *Toledo Blade* of their narrow escape. "I saw [the other] truck flipped over by the wind, and then it was me. Up in the air I went and over on the side. I'm sure," he continued, "the radio station just said the big blow was over, the tornado alert had ended, but not for us."

It was also not over for the passengers of a Short Way Lines bus. Ironically the New York Central Railroad had chartered the bus to take crew members and passengers of one of their trains to Detroit after storm debris blocked NYC tracks in Indiana. Four of the eleven passengers were dead at the scene. A fifth died a few days later. One railroad employee said the bus flipped around "like a roller coaster. I've spent forty-two years working for the railroad," he went on, "and I have to get hurt seriously in a bus." Another passenger said they had been tossed around "as though we were in a box being shaken up." Then all was quiet and "pitch black." He lay there until "someone shined a flashlight into the bus and I saw a window through which I could crawl."

That flashlight belonged to Isadore Perlmutter. He and his wife, Marian, were on their way home to Toledo from Detroit, where they had attended a wedding. They had remained, visiting relatives, until they heard the "all clear" notice on television. Nearing Toledo they realized all was not clear. Traffic stopped, and their car rocked. It was dark, and, "We didn't realize it was a tornado," Perlmutter recalls. They remained in place about fifteen minutes before traffic slowly began to move. Continuing south, "There were wrecks all over the place." One, on the median, stood out. "I saw a head and shoulders sticking out of this vehicle," Perlmutter says. It was the driver of the bus, who said he had been there for twenty minutes waiting for help. "My back is gone," the man said. Perlmutter put him in his car and started for a hospital, but the vehicle became stuck in the muddy median. He stopped another car, and its driver agreed to take the man to the hospital. He later died. Perlmutter returned to the bus, shined his flashlight in an opening, and people began to crawl out. With that, others stopped to help. "It was a horrible night," Marian says. "He was helping people, and I was screaming." They were actually lucky to be where they were. "If it would have been two cars sooner," Perlmutter reflects, "I don't know."[6]

East of the expressway, at her home on North Summit Street, Barbara (Hugill) Jones listened to a police scanner that "was really popping," and watched as countless ambulances and all forms of emergency vehicle went past. The many wrecks had blocked I-75, and Summit Street became the access route to Creekside Addition, a housing development, that, in a night replete with hideous scenes, would go down as one of the worst. The *Blade* was not exaggerating when it said the neighborhood, "resembles a bombed-out area."[7]

The home of Gene and Betty Cerveny, located on Vistamor Road, was at the edge of it. They had put their four children to bed and might have been in bed themselves had it not been for Betty's father, who lived with them at the time. He was watching Bonanza, the show of choice, it seems, for 1965 tornado victims, and he asked them to watch it with him. As Ben and the boys dealt with their weekly crisis, it began to rain. It grew harder, and wind accompanied it. The Cervenys went upstairs to shut windows just as it hit. The force of the wind pushed Gene to the upstairs floor. He managed to make it to his daughter's bedroom, reaching to grab her hand as she reached out to him. Then both were again pushed to the floor, looking up to see the roof lift, twirl, and disappear. Betty had the same sensation of being pushed down as she got to one of their son's bedroom. Yet from somewhere a light emerged, allowing him to see as his mother helped him to the floor. Betty describes the sound as that of "a big freight train," Gene as that of "a hundred jets."

They got all of the kids to the basement. Then, aware that neighbors had to be injured, Gene went up to the couple's bedroom to get some blankets. He opened the door, and the bedroom was not there. "Had we gone to bed rather than going down to see Bonanza...," he says, needing to say no more. One of those injured neighbors arrived at their door. He was an Episcopal priest, bloodied, wearing only his undershorts. Gene offered first to pray with him, but the dazed clergyman, whose family was missing, replied, "God damn it, who has time to pray at a time like this?" Gene and Betty went to help him search. His mother-in-law was killed, but the others were found alive, his baby in a pocket of debris. The Cervenys helped throughout the night. It was a large task. Every house north of theirs for a distance of about twenty-five homes was destroyed. It was also a dangerous undertaking. Only later did Gene think about the dangers of downed power lines. At the time he was concentrating on carrying mud-caked bodies to ambulances, not knowing if the people he bore were alive or dead. The Cervenys' home was about a foot off its foundation. It had to be leveled and rebuilt. While it was they stayed in the home of a family from their church who went away each summer. A neighboring family, Gene recalls, "lived on pills" out of nervousness for several months. Their cure finally came when they built a storm shelter.[8]

Another neighbor, Paul D. Smith, fared much worse. The day before, Smith and his wife, Shirley, had celebrated their eleventh anniversary. That night he worked the late shift for the Norfolk & Western Railroad, getting home Sunday morning. Daughter Sherrie, 8, and son Paul, 6, were home. The Smiths' youngest child, John, age two, was staying with neighbors so Shirley could more easily recuperate from recent surgery. Television told of a tornado near Van Wert. Soon it began to storm in Toledo. It scared his son, but Smith calmed him by saying there was nothing to worry about. "I felt guilty about that afterward," he says.

It was windy, "then, just like that, no wind. I said, 'uh-oh,'" Smith recalls. He went upstairs to get the kids. As he did he saw a bedroom window crash. Then: "Noise. I don't know how to explain it. I was in a vacuum and I was flying." He landed in a neighbor's driveway. His shoes were gone, and "it was so cold." Smith started back to where his house had been. At times he could see things; at times he could not. On the way he found a car with a little girl next to it, unconscious. He placed the girl in the car to keep her dry. Neighbors later got her to a hospital, and she recovered. Smith, too, was hospitalized. He remained in the hospital for two weeks. "I thought my neck was broken," he says, a self-diagnosis that was confirmed thirty years later. He had a severe cut on his jaw, and the muscles in his left shoulder were torn loose. When he arrived, the man in the next bed had a transistor radio and was listening to news about the storm. One item was personal: the broadcaster announced that Smith's wife had been killed.

The Night of the Wicked Winds 51

Debris covered Paul Smith's car in Toledo's Creekside Addition. (Paul Smith)

President Lyndon Johnson inspects the damage at Creekside Addition. (Paul Smith)

His children had all been blown out of the house. Sherrie went with the beds, ending up between two mattresses and suffering only a fractured ankle. The wind carried Paul two houses away and would have taken him farther had he not struck the woman who lived there, bruising her shoulder. The house where John was staying was also destroyed. The couple was upstairs when the tornado lifted their roof and them with it. The lady of the house was injured when a chest of drawers came down on her as they landed. It took some time for rescuers to find John. A fireman finally did, mistaking the infant at first for a clump of dirt. His skull had been severely crushed, and a portion of his leg was dangling. Rescuers actually wrapped that portion around the stump to keep him from bleeding to death. At the hospital doctors amputated the mangled leg, cleaned him up, then, realizing they could do no more, waited for him to die. "But I surprised them," John later wrote. After several months in the hospital he went home. He returned to have a rib removed and inserted where a portion of skull was missing. He also had to adjust to an artificial leg. "I learned how to live my daily life just like everybody else," he wrote, "with one exception: I had to put my leg on every morning."[9]

Beyond Creekside Addition, more destruction occurred along Shoreland Avenue, which hugs the west bank of the Ottawa River. Among those losing their homes were a sixty-one-year old man and his wife. The couple was at home when the tornado hit, huddling together in a corner of their kitchen. "I thought it was the end," the man told the *Blade*. "I even said good-bye to my wife." He was nearly right. The wind blew their house into the river, forcing them to climb over the breakwater to escape. The couple had numerous cuts and abrasions, but they were not seriously injured. "Here's my wardrobe," the man said as he displayed boots, a pair of trousers, and a sheet. "Everything else is at the bottom of the river."[10]

Less than a block away, at an area then known as McLeary's Point, Bill and Nancy Schill had returned from Adrian, Michigan, where they had served as Godparents for their niece. "It was a beautiful day," Nancy remembers, "warm, wonderful." Nancy had to be at work at six o'clock the next morning. She went to bed early, but Bill stayed up. She is not sure if she ever fell asleep, but remembers a storm containing "unbelievable" lightning. Suddenly, Bill bolted into the bedroom, shouting, "Get up, there's a tornado coming." He wanted her under the piano, and she reluctantly complied. With that it hit. The next thing she remembers was "sliding, things falling on me, and whirling" as the storm sucked her and Bill from under the piano and tossed them through the air. "It was split second," she emphasizes. "It all happened so fast." Unlike so many others, Nancy adds, "I never remembered the noise at all." Bill later told Don Loucks, a friend of the couple, that he remembered the same sensations of sliding and flying while being struck with debris.

The Schills ended up behind where their house had been. They had been blown in reverse of the direction of the storm's path. Their house was gone, the kitchen sent forward into the river. "I remember being cold and wet," Nancy says, "then the pain." She had been unconscious, although she feels not for long, and she had no idea what had happened. What she did know was that her foot was bleeding, and the injury seemed serious. Bill and Nancy were close together. One of them called out to the other; Nancy isn't sure which one. Their car was still there, but finding the keys was not possible, so Bill, unaware that his back had been injured, started to carry Nancy to locate help. Fortunately someone came by in a jeep. He wrapped Nancy in a blanket and took them both to Riverside Hospital utilizing side roads and fields. The scene there was one of hectic confusion; Bill ended up receiving several tetanus shots that night.

Don Loucks visited the couple in the hospital. Bill, he remembers, looked as though someone had taken a needle and scraped at different lengths all over his body. From his hospital bed, Bill asked Loucks to see if he could find any of the couple's possessions. He went, accompanied by his brother, Bob, and Ray Tarr, a friend. The three could not locate anything. Later two folding chairs and some silver dollars were recovered. The Schills' pool table was never found. In a neighboring home, Loucks recalls, chards of glass in the walls showed the pattern of the funnel.

The Schills remained in the hospital several weeks. Nancy had a broken ankle and a badly lacerated foot. The scar would remain with her. Bill had numerous small cuts and a serious one on his left arm. He suffered from frequent panic attacks in the months that followed, although treatment gradually eased them. The ordeal also "changed our attitudes about things," Nancy says. The couple thought more about life and eventually adopted two children. "You find out," she says, "that things [possessions] aren't important."[11]

It's a long way from Grayling Place in northwestern Toledo to Shoreland, and the distance was much more daunting on the evening of April 11, 1965. That, however, was the path Sam "Bud" Foreman followed. It was a journey that began out of curiosity and ended out of a commitment to helping others. Foreman was working in his garage with a friend when what he thought was a strong storm blew through. It began, he recalls with high winds followed by hail and then "a tremendous roar." His wife, Sandy, and their four children were visiting with his father-in-law. Foreman called and was reassured that all were well. He learned, however, that the Glass Bowl had sustained damage. Foreman and his friend drove there to check out the situation. Seeing the damaged building and cars in the parking lot with their windows gone, the men "began to get the idea" that the storm had been a tornado.

54   *The Night of the Wicked Winds*

Remains of the Bill and Nancy Schill home at Shoreland. (Nancy Schill)

What was left of the piano under which Bill and Nancy Schill took refuge. (Nancy Schill)

Two views of damaged homes along Toledo's Shoreland Avenue. (Don Loucks)

They continued on to Foreman's father-in-law's home, where they heard vague reports about Shoreland being hit. The pair went to help. Upon arriving the Red Cross gave them arm bands, and they started through the neighborhood with flashlights, searching through homes and basements for victims. "Everything was flattened," Foreman remembers. "This area was gone, almost like a level field." Without street lights, he adds, "it seemed pitch dark." He could hear natural gas escaping from broken lines. Otherwise, "the quiet was dominating." Coming from one home, Foreman "saw what I thought was a rug rolled up against a curb." Upon examination it turned out to be the lifeless body of an elderly woman. She was covered in dirt "like she'd been rolled in cinders." The body was some distance from the nearest home site, and "the treachery she must have gone through" troubled Foreman immensely.

At another spot Foreman found a rifle inside a weapon bag. He tried to turn it in to officials, but the Red Cross "wouldn't have anything to do with it." Neither would anyone else, producing "a little bit of frustration." He did not want to carry it around, nor did he want to leave it. Finally a police lieutenant agreed to relieve him of the weapon.[12]

Two people died on Lost Peninsula, a strip of land between the Ottawa River and Maumee Bay. A quirk of geography put the northern tip of the peninsula in Monroe County Michigan, although it is only accessible by road through Ohio. Both deaths occurred in the Michigan section. One victim, Mrs. Irma Lashaway, had been Miss Toledo in 1937. Emergency crews rushing to the area found their way blocked by the remains of a tavern blown across Edgewater Drive at the state line. Bulldozers were pressed into service to clear the way. The storm tossed pleasure boats around like toys. One rested on top of a house. Another, a 25-foot cruiser, could not be found. Monroe County Sheriff Charles G. Harrington told the *Monroe Evening News* that twenty-seven of forty homes on the peninsula "were demolished," and forty cars were either damaged or destroyed. The wind threw one car 500 feet. Twenty-nine residents were injured.[13]

One man told the *News* that he heard a noise "like an explosion." He ran upstairs to check on his five children and discovered that his roof was gone. None of the children was hurt. A few houses away the wind left only two walls of a brick home standing. "All I saw," the owner said, "was the roof of my house coming down." The pressure knocked him to the floor, but he somehow escaped injury. Fred Abair and his wife, Bernadine, were watching television with their children and visitors that evening. He heard wind and walked into the kitchen to look out the window. "Then," he says, "the glass started leaving the house and the thing hit." At the Abair home, too, no one was hurt seriously. Their roof was gone, however, and their visitors' Oldsmobile was leaning against the house.[14]

It was, Dick Rombkowski remembers, a calm, "almost motionless" night at his home just over the Michigan border on Lost Peninsula. Dick had planned to go to a party that evening with his brother, but his mother, sister, and three nieces were visiting. The brothers flipped a coin, and Dick ended up at home with the relatives. Late in the evening Rombkowski left for a brief visit with a neighbor couple, leaving his family members at his place. As his neighbor opened the door, "It sounded like a locomotive was bearing down on us." The neighbor lay atop his wife and their infant child, and Rombkowski headed for the back door. He planned to run back home, but with all the windows breaking, he too went for the floor. "I wish I could explain how I felt," he says, adding, "I don't think there's a more helpless feeling in the whole world." As he lay there, "numb and powerless," bricks from the chimney struck his head.

When he stood up both his home and his neighbors' house were gone, as were four others in an area about 200 yards by 100. Rombkowski headed for home to check on his family. It was still extremely windy, and he remembers being lifted and dropped as he ran. At the house Rombkowski's twin nieces Karen (Beale) Skelton and Kim (Beale) Johnson, then five years old, and younger sister Chere`, only six weeks old, had survived the storm. So, too, had their mother, Ruth Beale, and their grandmother, Irene Laderach. The girls were unhurt, but both their mother and their grandmother were badly injured.

Mrs. Beale and the girls were staying with Rombkowski as their family prepared to move from California to Ohio. Two older half sisters, Cindy (Klockowski) Roach, and Debbie Klockowski, were staying with their grandparents in south Toledo. Cindy and Debbie, along with a cousin, had spent Palm Sunday visiting with their sisters and mother. They wanted to spend the night, but Monday was a school day, and their grandparents wanted them to return.

Kim recalls watching the news and the television picture becoming snowy. Karen remembers rain and lightning, then lights flickering and a strong wind. Then there was a loud rumble "like a train," glass breaking, and people screaming. "Before I knew it," she says, "everything was down." Their mother put the two girls in the fireplace as the tornado approached. Their grandmother, who thought the commotion portended the end of the world, lay atop Chere` on a couch. When it was over the fireplace was virtually all that remained of the house. Rombkowski's Thunderbird had landed on the twins' bed, resting upon its roof.

His house gone and the rain still falling, Dick found things to cover everyone. Then, joined by the neighbor he had planned to visit, he went to check on others. Their shoes were gone, so the men put purses they found on their feet to avoid glass. They propped up the roof of a nearby house that appeared to have imploded. The next house was the one in which Irma Lashaway was killed. At the next a couple crawled into a small wine cellar. Had they not, they would likely have not survived; the cement slab was all that remained of their home. Next door, a couple dived under a pool table in their sub-basement. The tornado took their home and dumped in water from the Ottawa River. They nearly drowned, but managed to escape. Rombkowski and his neighbor walked half a mile before they came to a house with lights on. From there they called for help. It took about two and one-half hours for the first ambulance to arrive. As he waited, Rombkowski watched looters descend on the neighborhood, but did nothing, "not that I was scared [of them], I just didn't care."

As her uncle carried her outside, Kim says, "I remember the screaming and the sirens," along with a "parade of ambulances." Overturned cars garnished the neighborhood. Her grandmother was placed into an ambulance, "shaking as if she was freezing." In protecting the girls both she and Mrs. Beale were bombarded with glass. More serious, an iron partition hit their mother in the head and knocked her out. With a blood clot near her brain, she faced several weeks in the hospital. Arriving there that night, Mrs. Beale had the added ordeal of dealing with a woman who wanted to take Chere` from her. The woman's baby was missing, and, in her traumatized condition, she became convinced that Chere` was her daughter. Cindy visited her mother the next day but did not recognize her because of the cuts and bruises on her face. "That is not my mother," she thought upon arriving. "It was a very devastating thing to see."

The devastation remained. The sisters all admit to being "hysterical" for many years after when storms threatened. Even after the passage of nearly four decades they still become nervous.[15]

5

"Then, All of a Sudden, KABOOM!"

Shelby County

The Shelby County tornado touched down a short distance southwest of Fort Loramie at about 10:00 p.m. It grazed the southern edge of that community as it headed northeast before turning almost due east along Fort-Loramie-Swanders Road. Later the twister paralleled Meranda Road. Its path was through farm country, although it came perilously close to the villages of Anna, Swanders, and Maplewood. The tornado missed Sidney, the county seat, by only about four miles. This kept the death toll relatively low. A seventy-five-year old woman living on the Schmitmeyer-Baker Road near Minster died of head and abdominal injuries after her house collapsed upon her. The storm also killed a brother and sister, aged ninety and eighty-four, on Meranda Road near Maplewood.[1]

Shelby County Sheriff Robert Burns told the *Sidney Daily News* that the tornado hit "at least" 150 farms. Its winds destroyed twenty-four homes, thirty-eight barns, and eighty-eight other buildings. An additional thirty-one homes, twenty barns, and thirteen other buildings sustained varying degrees of damage. At one farm alone on Harmon Road the tornado "flattened or seriously damaged" the house and twelve other structures. Over one hundred cattle and 125 hogs were killed or had to be destroyed, and local officials warned motorists to be alert to roaming livestock. Two Fort Loramie businesses were destroyed, an auto body shop and a bulk fertilizer plant. Thirty automobiles were damaged beyond repair. Just north of Swanders the winds blew fifty-three cars of a northbound Baltimore & Ohio freight train off the track, forcing the B&O to reroute trains over an alternate route.[2]

Among the first Shelby County residents to experience the twister were Martin and Melba Bender, their children, Joyce (Porter), Bonnie (Josefovsky), Dan, and Roger, and the nearly fifty people who were at their home that night. The Benders were in the process of moving, and their friends and neighbors surprised them with a going away party. The second surprise came shortly before ten o'clock when Martin heard doors banging on outbuildings. Roger recalls that his father went out to latch the doors and spotted a funnel west of the barn. He emphasizes, however, along with his mother and sisters, that this was not the destructive F4 that devastated the county. That storm, Bender says, came "at least fifteen minutes" later and was much louder. It chased the group to the basement. Bonnie and Joyce remember the windows ripling first. "Then," Bonnie says, "there was this big boom." With that everyone headed to the cellar. Bonnie knew the situation was serious when a neighbor said, "We must pray." With that she started to cry as Dan put his arms around her and said, "Don't worry; it'll be O. K."

He was right, at least in terms of the house and its many occupants. Outside there was considerable damage. All of the guests' cars, some twenty-five, were damaged, at least half to the point that they could not be driven. In addition a large apple tree blocked the Benders' dead end road. Parents, worried about their children at home, were frantic. Some walked home. One of them went to the home of "the local drunk," who happened to own the only chain saw in the neighborhood. The group cleared the tree, and by 4:00 a.m. the Benders knew that none of their guests had lost any family members.

The Benders had held a farm sale the day before, which limited their loss somewhat. Most livestock and equipment were no longer there when the storm hit. Their orchard, however, remained, and about twenty trees were down after the storm. The barn was destroyed. The three milk cows that had been inside were found about fifty feet away from the wreckage with only minor scratches. Martin raised purebred Duroc hogs. He found a breeding boar some sixteen hours after the storm, pinned beneath a beam. Martin sold it, and the man who purchased it later said it was the best breeding boar he ever had. The Benders found not a trace of a twelve-by-sixteen-foot portable sow hut. However, its straw nests were still in place, undisturbed. The family's dog was found quivering under a 1953 Ford tractor that had been in a lean-to attached to the destroyed barn. From that day on, whenever a storm approached, the dog sought out the tractor, even if it was way off in a field, and took shelter beneath it. Like the dog, the Bender family had been relatively lucky. Still, Melba's father summed up the situation succinctly when he told his daughter Monday morning, "Sis, you throw one hell of a party."[3]

Working at his family's service station in Fort Loramie, Tim Ernst had noticed skies that were "unusually eerie" with "weird colors." He was home by the time the storm hit, its path about one-fourth of a mile away. It took the house and all the buildings on his grandparents' farm, where his aunt and uncle, Sis and Leo Goubeaux, lived with their six children. "There was just nothing there but splintered wood and boards," he says. Despite the fact that the home did not have a basement, none of the family was seriously hurt. The next farm, however, was the scene of one of Shelby County's three fatalities.[4]

"It sounded like a train in the yard," says Don Puthoff, who lived about three miles east of Fort Loramie. He looked out the front door and saw the funnel north of his home and his car blown off the driveway and against a poultry house. "It happened so quick and was so disruptive I didn't know what was happening," Puthoff notes. His wife, Phyl, was standing in the kitchen, holding the couple's one-month old daughter. Their black terrier was standing nearby. Suddenly the dog jumped and Phyl found herself holding him as well. The storm door blew in, showering two girls sitting on a couch with glass but leaving them uncut. The Puthoffs' other daughter had just gone to bed. Jeannie (Puthoff) Snarr remembers a storm accompanied by hail that suddenly went silent. "Then," she says, "you heard the noise and I didn't know what the heck was going on."

Don and Phyl went next door to check on Don's parents. They were unhurt, but their home was damaged beyond repair, twisted and knocked off its foundation. A 1948 tornado had taken all the buildings except their house. This one completed the task. Don and Phyl lost "at least" one hundred turkeys. Their poultry house roof had a hole in it, and dead turkeys were sucked out and found on Route 29, six miles away. For the next several days they had to haul water to keep the other five to six thousand birds alive. They also hauled sixteen wagon loads of trash from their woods, aided by "neighbors we never even knew." The porch of their home was misaligned, and their front door and windows were out.[5]

Tom R. Niekamp had been visiting relatives in Dayton with his wife, Mary, and their children, Daniel and Angela. The family left about 7:30 for their home in Chickasaw. As they exited I-75 and traveled northwest on Route 29 there was lightning followed by rain. The rain became torrential. Ahead of them they made out tail lights, then brake lights. Suddenly things became still, and the car was blown sideways. About five seconds later the wind lifted the front of the car and blew the vehicle end over end into a field. Tom and Angela, who was one year old, were blown from the car. "She was crying her head off," recalls Niekamp, who was awakened by the sound. He went to the car and yelled, helping Daniel out before Mary crawled from the vehicle.

The other car was still on the road. As the young women who were in it walked to find help, the Niekamps crawled back into their car to escape the rain. Two teenagers came by and took the family to the Wilson Memorial Hospital in Sidney. Daniel had bad cuts on his arm and chest. There was glass in Angela's knee. Mary's shoulder was badly bruised, and Tom had dirt in his eye. They spent the night in the Sidney hospital and three more days in a hospital in Coldwater. A month later Tom received a package in the mail. It was his wallet, found by a farmer some three miles away.[6]

Jon Blakley was also on the road that night. The Capital University student, on spring break, was returning to his home north of Sidney after visiting friends. On the way he saw a friend walking home from work and offered her a ride. "I was completely blind sided," Blakley says. "It wasn't even raining [at that time]." His first sign of trouble was static on the radio. Then the rain began, just a sprinkle at first, then a downpour. "I couldn't see past the windshield," he notes, so he stopped the car just short of an intersection. When the rain let up a bit, Blakley continued to the intersection and turned left onto Harmon Road. He got a short distance before the rain again intensified, forcing him to stop the car once more. Some thirty seconds later a gust of wind blew the rear of the car into a ditch and sent something crashing through the rear window.

Then, Blakley says, "it just got dead calm for about ten seconds." Suddenly the wind resumed, things began hitting the car, and the front end of the vehicle lifted. Instinctively he hit the brakes and tried to steer, but by then he was totally airborne. The car rolled, finally coming to rest 150 feet to the south. The wind was over, but there was still rain. Blakley's first thought was that he must get help for his injured passenger. His second was, "How is my dad going to believe the wind did this?" He dealt with the initial problem first, walking toward I-75 past sparking wires for help. He came to a house, but the residents could not help him find aid. Their telephone was out and the garage had collapsed on top of their car. Continuing on, Blakley met a car. His passenger was inside, remembering nothing of what had happened. She had a broken collar bone, cuts, and bruises. Blakley was also cut and bruised, along with a compression fracture of two vertebrae. He also made the *Sidney Daily News* as Shelby County's first looting victim when someone removed the spare tire from his car.[7]

One of the most miraculous stories of survival occurred on Meranda Road, some four miles west of Maplewood, at the home of James and Betty Riggs and their seven children. One of those seven, Robert, remembers being in bed "bawling my eyes out" because the storm scared him. His father, he recalls, paddled him to make him be quiet. "The next thing I remember," Robert notes, "is he picked us up out of a field." Robert and brothers James Jr., Kenneth, John, and Jerry were all in bed upstairs when the tornado struck their two-story frame house. James and Betty were downstairs with the two youngest children, Rita and Jeffrey. Betty remembers hearing the noise and her husband shouting, "Oh no!" as he grabbed the two youngsters and jumped onto the bed with her. Her next memory is being outside, still on the mattress, and James yelling for her. James recalls a "big boom when the window popped," spinning, and letting loose of the mattress. Then he was fifty feet from the house, and "everything was over me." He kicked debris away to get up and took a census of his children, scattered in the fields, with the aid of lightning flashes. James Jr., the oldest, walked over to his father. Jerry was found last, perhaps a half hour later. As James located them, he took the kids to Betty, who put them in the family car. Robert recalls that he was blown three hundred feet west. James Jr. went straight up, landing gently in the driveway. The others were taken in all directions.

Jon Blakley's car, which the twister lifted in Shelby County. (Jon Blakley)

After the family was together they began walking down the road, their car being in no shape to travel. The kids held hands and walked in groups of two as their father warned them to watch out for downed wires. They hiked nearly a mile before a man picked the family up and took them to the hospital in Sidney. With two deep cuts in his head, Robert was the most seriously injured. Everyone except Rita and Jeffrey required stitches. Betty was well enough that she volunteered to help other patients at the hospital.

Their rented home was entirely gone, and the landlord lost a number of cattle and chickens. People living four and five miles away returned family pictures. The employees of Copeland Refrigeration, where James worked, took up a collection and bought Easter clothes for the family. A local realtor let the Riggses live in a home he was offering for sale until they relocated.[8]

Roger Lantz and his brother, Gary, took a nephew to a drive-in movie at Sidney Palm Sunday evening. They left at about ten o'clock, before the movie ended, because of rain, wind, and lightning. Roger and Gary worked in partnership on their parents' dairy farm about nine miles east of Fort Loramie. Approaching home on Route 29 they noticed large electric poles leaning. As they continued poles were on the ground. About a fourth of a mile from their farm the poles blocked the road. They began walking. Through the lightning, Roger recalls, they noticed that their buildings were considerably lower than they should have been. All of them, it turned out, had been leveled.

64   *The Night of the Wicked Winds*

The Schitmeyer farm, located on Route 29, in Shelby County. (Shelby County Historical Society)

Barn damage at the Shelby County farm of W. A. Lochard. (SCHS)

Debris wrapped around a Shelby County fence post. (SCHS)

Unidentified rural home in western Shelby County. (SCHS)

Farm damage in western Shelby County. (Shelby County Historical Society)

Several animals were trapped inside the buildings, and with the help of neighbors, the family worked until 4:00 a.m. to get them out. They lost six cattle and a few pigs, a much smaller loss than they had initially feared. Their house was still standing, but it had moved eight inches on its foundation. Lantz's parents later told him the house had seemed to float. The power had remained on until the tornado struck. The clock stopped at 10:11.[9]

Phyllis Lackey lived with her husband and their five children northeast of Maplewood just over the Logan County line. Palm Sunday, she says, was hot and humid, "one of those days that you want to get away from." That night there was thunder, then wind, and a downpour of rain that "just beat on the house." Phyllis went to bed about ten while her husband and the children stayed up to watch television. At one point he came into the room and asked how she could sleep during such a storm. Phyllis had just taken a class called, "Cast your care upon God." She replied, "I've already prayed about it," rolled over, and went back to sleep.

The next morning a neighbor asked her if she wanted to go for a ride to survey the storm damage. That was the first she had heard of it. Phyllis went along, viewing scenes and hearing stories that were hard for her to believe. Most buildings along the path, she noticed, were wiped out, and debris littered the fields. Most stunning was the realization that the storm had turned about one-half mile from her home and lifted. "When that hit me," Phyllis confesses, "I was putty for several days."[10]

Union, Delaware, and Morrow Counties

About an hour and a half after Shelby County's tornado touched down, another twister reached the ground in extreme eastern Union County. It continued east-northeast through Thompson, Radnor, Marlboro, and Oxford Townships in Delaware County then roared into Morrow County. Three deaths were directly attributable to the tornado. A fourth, a heart attack victim, was likely produced by the storm. "It was a hell of a night," the fire chief in the tiny village of Radnor told the *Columbus Dispatch*. He and his twenty-man department had worked from 11:30 Sunday night well into Monday afternoon, going from house to house searching for victims. Ambulances followed the firemen. They delivered twenty-four residents to various hospitals.[11]

Pat Spriggs was at her Radnor home with sons Gene, Rex, and Donald the night "hell broke loose." Her husband, Don, was on his way home from Indiana with a truckload of chickens, following storms as he went. Indeed, by the time he arrived hail had killed all the chickens in the top level. The sound of things hitting their concrete block home was Pat's first sign that something was amiss. Then all the living room windows suddenly broke. Pat ran to check on the boys, sitting with them against a bed, trying to shelter them. "I just sat there and waited," she recalls. Pat continued to wait after the storm had passed, anxious for rescuers to arrive. "It seemed like it took forever for someone to come and get us," she says, adding that this likely was not the case. Radnor firemen had taken her and the boys to another home by the time Don arrived at midnight. Not knowing that, he struggled mightily to reach his house. It took four policemen and firefighters to hold him back and keep him from charging through downed power lines.

Returning to her demolished home the next morning, Pat realized how lucky she was that she had chosen to wait up for her husband. A wall had fallen, flattening the couple's bed. They found the refrigerator door closed, but items from it were scattered. The clothes iron Pat had placed on the stove to cool was found in the oven. Their 1955 Pontiac Chieftain was blown over a four-foot fence, landing one hundred feet away. Their dog was dead, his back broken by debris. The Spriggses recovered very few possessions, but they did find papers from Indiana. They received a great deal of assistance from the Red Cross, including clothing for the boys and furniture. "I don't know what we'd have done without the Red Cross," Pat says. The family rebuilt, and on April 11, 1966, the one year anniversary of the tornado, they lost everything again in a house fire.[12]

Don R. Stutler lived with his parents, Don and Mary, on Jones Road, about a mile northeast of Radnor. As the storm intensified, Mary awakened him and his father. The three heard an "ungodly roar" as something crashed through a window and struck Stutler's mother, cutting her face and knocking her unconscious. She fell into Don's arms as the tornado struck their home. It picked up the house, Stutler says, "and we just rolled down to the foundation." As they did a coal stove fell over, leaving all three with burns. Stutler clambered out of the debris and went to find help. In the meantime members of the fire department arrived and summoned an ambulance. The crew carried Mrs. Stutler some distance because downed trees and power lines blocked the road. She would remain in the hospital a week. Stutler and his father were released that evening. Their one-story house was gone, along with most of its contents. Don's basketball was later found along U. S. Route 23, some five miles away.[13]

Nearby, about a mile and a half northeast of Radnor, David and Vicki James were at home with their two-year old son, Mark, and daughter, Lori Ann, who was four months old. The family had returned from visiting Vicki's parents in Marion, driving through lightning the entire way. They decided to wait until the storm passed to put the children to bed. At 11:17 the electricity went off. A minute later Vicki said her ears felt as if they were ready to pop from extreme pressure. With that David shouted for her to get to the floor. He sheltered Mark, as she covered Lori Ann. While they were down, it felt to Vicki as if the door had come open. "I thought if I could get to that door and shut it," she says, "I'd be fine." She got up to close it, but David pulled her back down. The door had not come open. The house was gone.

After the tornado passed, David recalls, he and Vicki looked "like someone took a shotgun full of glass and shot us. We were mud and blood from head to foot." A chair had struck Vicki in the back, and a window frame had hit David's head. Lori, they later learned, had glass in her ear canal. Fearful that a ceiling or wall would collapse, David's first thought was to get out of the house. Their home was off its foundation, and they had to step across the gap onto the porch. One side of their car was caved in, and a beam was through the back window. They got in anyway to escape the cold. Soon after they saw headlights. It was David's father and brother coming to check on them. His brother ruined his car driving over debris to reach the family and get them to help. He took them to David's parents' home, where they cleaned themselves up somewhat. David later returned to help search for missing neighbors. As he did a telephone line caught him in the neck, injuring him further. He also learned that he had lost nearly sixty hogs to the storm. "Every time it would lightning," he recalls, "you'd see dead hogs lying everywhere."

Daylight, of course, revealed even more destruction, as well as a number of looters. David returned the next morning to discover both looters and people trying to chase them away. He found several pigeons virtually dressed clean and skillets embedded in trees. The tornado had sucked the tile from a portion of the kitchen floor, but a bowl of fruit on the kitchen table was not disturbed. Their home was far beyond repair, and six other buildings were lost. One, a metal corn crib, was "a mangled ball" three-fourths of a mile away from its original location. Worse, the Jameses spent April 14, their wedding anniversary, attending funerals. It was an experience, David notes, that stayed with the residents of Delaware County. Nine years later about thirty of them headed a few miles southwest to do what they could to help. Their destination: Xenia.[14]

George W. and Fern Thomas lived just east of the Jameses on Price Road. One-fourth of a mile south their son, George R. Thomas, was watching television with his wife, Mary Anne, as their four children slept upstairs. They learned of tornadoes to the north just before the lights went out. A short time later, George R. heard a noise and thought, "That freight train sounds awfully loud." He dashed upstairs and brought the kids down to the kitchen. Looking out the north window he saw the barn "all scrunched over." He then looked toward his parents' home and noticed a flashing light and buildings that were "disarrayed."

One of those disarrayed buildings had been his parents' home since 1926. The tornado leveled the two-story house to within about three feet from the ground. The couple had dashed for an east bedroom as the storm approached, but they did not make it. George W. grabbed his wife and held her so tightly that he broke three of her ribs. He regained consciousness fifty feet from the house site, beneath a bedroom floor. The bed had remained in place as the floor blew out from under it. Mr. Thomas extricated himself from the debris by clutching the door of a refrigerator that had been two rooms away. He then freed his wife. George R. took them both, along with neighbor R. Bruce McKibben, to Grady Hospital in Delaware. His father, with a partially paralyzed leg, remained in the hospital for two weeks. His mother was a patient for three weeks. They fared better than a school bus body that George W., a bus dealer, had in the yard. It was blown half a mile away, hitting on one end and then the other until it was crumpled, George R. says, "to about six feet, just like an accordion."[15]

This picture, taken near Radnor, appeared on the cover of the May 1965 *Country Living*, the magazine of Ohio rural electric co-ops. (*Country Living*)

As for R. Bruce McKibben, the neighbor who went to the hospital with the Thomases, his story is one of the most tragic of all those coming out of the Palm Sunday storms, and it could have been worse. "Had it not been for Fritz," he says, "I wouldn't be here." A high school student, seventeen years old, McKibben lived with his parents, Richard and Marjorie McKibben, on County Road 8 about four miles northeast of Radnor. Fritz was his dog. McKibben was sitting in the family room with his father when the lights went off during a pouring rain. "I said I was going to go outside and unhook my dog," he recalls. To avoid getting wet he entered the garage from the house and opened the door from the inside. Fritz slipped under, and Bruce lowered the door. His first, brief, sign of trouble came when the door began "waffling."

"Then, all of a sudden, KABOOM!"

Remembering a riot he had seen, Bruce rolled himself into a ball for protection. His next memory is waking up some twenty to twenty-five feet away, straight north. "I had a pile of cement blocks on me," he says. They came from the garage. His first instinct was to remain where he was, but, "Something said, 'No, don't lay there,' so I got up." He walked toward where the garage had been. A propitious lightning flash kept him from falling into the basement of what had been his home. He could see that both his home and his neighbors' were gone. Glenn and Bob James picked him up and took him to George R. Thomas's house. From there he went to the hospital.

"I was really beat up pretty good," McKibben says. A two-by-four was driven into his leg and up into his abdomen about eight inches. His back was totally lacerated. "You couldn't put a pin head on my back," he notes. The injuries kept him in the hospital for two weeks.

Both his parents were killed. "Dick" McKibben was the area's rural mail carrier. His mother-in-law, who was also his boss, told a reporter, "He was just a wonderful man." Paul Schlemmer of the *Columbus Dispatch* wrote, "Mrs. McKibben was a home economics teacher at Elgin High School in Marion County. She was a Sunday school teacher at the United Church of Christ. She was active in youth work. She was a lot of things to a lot of people."

His hospital stay spared Bruce from going through the clean-up process. He knew his house was "totally gone," and that the family's two cars, a Monterey and a Comet, were wrapped around trees about a hundred feet from where they had been parked. Bruce's grandfather found his class ring in a field. An ambulance bore him to the funeral home before the services for his parents took place, but he could remain only a few minutes. "It does make you grow up pretty fast," he says of the experience. For several months, he adds, people "walked on eggshells" when they were around him, not sure what to say. He lived with his grandmother and a great aunt. "You say, 'Well, you've just gotta move on,'" McKibben explains, although his aunt's ongoing displays of grief made it difficult for the youngster to put things behind him.

Fritz survived the storm.[16]

At 11:00 p.m. Palm Sunday night Dorothy Kaelber, a nurse's aide, checked in at Delaware's Grady Hospital for work. Normally she worked in the children's ward. That night she performed a variety of duties. Victims from Westfield, in Morrow County, arrived first, Dorothy says. One for whom she helped care was a baby found in a field on a refrigerator. The child was not badly hurt. Around 1:00 a.m., Dorothy recalls, "They started bringing in my neighbors." Phone lines were down, and she could not contact her family, who lived on a farm just west of U. S. 23.

Dorothy received permission to leave, although she does not remember driving home. Her next memory is driving into her yard and seeing her husband, Don, in the driveway. He reassured her that their three children, Dennis, Debbie, and Dianne, were fine. They were at a neighbor's house. Don had sensed trouble when he noticed a complete calm, "a silence you could feel," he explains. He hustled the kids to the basement and shoved them under a table. By then, Dennis adds, what had started as "a rumble in the west," had grown to a freight train sound, then to the roar of a jet.

After daylight Dorothy returned to a house garnished with glass and straw. A mattress was half way out a window, and curtains would never be found. Despite the mess, Dorothy made all the beds, feeling that there might be visitors. The house was off its foundation and had to be replaced. Three barns and various other outbuildings were gone. The Kaelbers lost eighteen hogs and all of their eighty to one hundred sheep. Neighbors helped cut cattle out of a barn, saving them all. Dennis remembers finding letters from Indiana and Illinois. Part of a round barn, Debbie (Kaelber) Caudill adds, was in the yard although nobody for miles around owned such a structure. Three hundred students from Columbus West High School arrived to clean the fields, and there was help from Amish groups and the Waldo Methodist Church. Despite their efforts, Don says, debris still in the fields produced over one hundred flat tires for tractors and machinery that summer.[17]

Nearby, John and Maxine Moore had returned home from visiting family in Guernsey County. Tired from the trip, John left the car out of the garage. The roar of the tornado awoke them, and they got their two children quickly to the basement. The family emerged to find two downstairs windows blown out and most of the shingles missing from their roof. A chicken house had blown over their car but missed it. The structure was in pieces in the garden. The Moores had two open hog houses a few feet apart. The wind lifted one and scattered the boards. The other remained in place. Pieces of wood were driven so far into the ground that John needed the tractor to extricate them. "People were so helpful," Maxine says of the clean-up effort. There were, she adds, numerous volunteer workers and canteens to feed them.[18]

Across Route 23 the storm hit Mom Wilson's Country Sausage, a well known area business. Sue (Wilson) Snavley recalls that her parents, Horace and Fern Wilson, had made a handshake agreement with the state a day or two earlier to sell some of their buildings for the expansion of the highway. That night Sue was in bed when she heard her mother say, "We need to go to the basement." She had heard something that sounded like a train go over the roof. Mr. Wilson remained upstairs, telling his wife when she returned, "Mom, I think we're wiped out." A plate glass window had been blown out of the business building, and an adjacent barn was leveled. Up the road some ten other buildings were gone. Six cattle were dead. Hogs had been blown across the road, but none were lost. The Wilson home was undamaged despite the fact that the wind had snapped off a utility pole next to it at the base.[19]

Gladys Geesey lost only a bit of the roof at her home on Route 257 south of Radnor, but she witnessed more destruction than almost anyone else in Delaware County. Gladys worked as a volunteer for the American Red Cross. Her job was to check on the injured and to determine what people's immediate needs were. Often people were too dazed to talk, she says, noting, "I had to look around and see for myself." Much of what she saw was disturbing. Along Route 203 homes were gone and there was "blood splattered all around." A lone brick wall was all that was standing at one home site. The lady living there had been in bed when the wind slammed her against the wall then deposited her back in bed. Straw protruded from utility poles, skillets from trees. At one location quart fruit jars were scattered everywhere. They remained intact, lids and all. Her experience left Gladys sure of one thing: "I don't want to see any more of them."[20]

From Delaware the tornado crossed into Morrow County, bearing down on the village of Westfield. It sounded, one resident told the *Morrow County Sentinel*, "like the buzzing of a million bees." Another told the *Marion Star*, "We thought it was an atomic bomb." A reporter from the paper wrote, "From every angle, [Westfield] resembled a junkyard." No one in the village was killed, but between twenty-two and twenty-six, depending on which press account one chooses to believe, were injured. This was out of a population of about one hundred. The community's general store was damaged, its township hall and the Methodist Church leveled. The storm destroyed sixteen houses and seriously damaged another sixteen. Just west of town one farmer lost six cattle and 125 chickens to the twister.[21]

Westfield residents Tom and Doris Crump went to a laundromat in Cardington every Sunday evening. Their seven children remained at home, with Noreena, age 16, in charge. She was particularly responsible for three-year old Andrew. With the lights flickering in Cardington, the

Crumps decided to return home, wet clothes and all. Coming down Morrow County road 156, they saw damaged homes and downed trees through lightning flashes. "Something's gone through here," Tom said. As they continued utility poles blocked the road, forcing them to make detours, or in some cases, get out and move them out of the way. At one point Doris actually lifted wires for Tom to drive under. Finally, less than a half mile from home, they came to an immovable object, a large maple tree, forcing them to walk the rest of the way.

Meanwhile, in their parents' absence, Noreena and her brother Keith, the next oldest, had seen their siblings through the crisis. It was a school night, and Noreena was considering going to bed when a strong wind caught her attention. She decided to close the picture window curtains. As she left the room, the window blew through. "We were trying to gather kids in all directions," Noreena (Crump) Taylor says of the next few moments. They herded them to the bathroom and put the smallest ones in the tub. "The noise was unreal," she remembers. "There's nothing in the world that sounds like a tornado hitting you." When the noise had passed, Noreena left the bathroom to investigate. She noticed the roof gone from a home across the street. A friend of hers lived there, and she rushed toward the home, only to be chased back by downed wires. She later learned that no one in the house had been badly hurt. Soon a neighbor woman came to check on the Crump children. It was about then, Noreena recalls, that she became very concerned for her parents' safety.

The feeling was mutual, but Tom and Doris soon returned to find their family alive and unhurt. Their home had not fared so well. Every window was broken except one, and a vandal tossed a brick through it the next night. Slate from a nearby roof was everywhere. One bedroom seemed to be filled with it. It took Tom about three months to repair the house. During that time the family lived in an apartment in the nearby community of Ashley. Their barn was gone. Only the door was found, six hundred feet away in a hedge fence. Also gone was a dog house, in which a goose had been sitting on eggs. They located the dog house a mile away. The eggs were scattered, but unbroken. As for the goose, she returned home two days later, minus her tail feathers.[22]

Three miles northeast of Westfield, Miriam Newell was at home with her seventeen-month old son, Larry. She had no idea what was about to hit their mobile home. She was with Larry in the bedroom when both were suddenly thrown into a corner. A mattress landed on top of them, which was fortunate. "I remember things hitting that mattress," she says. Their mobile home had been tossed five feet against an oak tree and an electric pole. Miriam threw a pillow through a broken window and dropped Larry on it, prompting him to giggle. Then she climbed out and went to the home of a neighbor. That house had been blown from its foundation, and her neighbor's leg was badly cut.

As all this happened, Miriam's husband, Cecil, working a few miles south, knew nothing of the tornado. Trees blocked his way home, however, and he began to walk, shouting for his wife as he went. Once they were reunited they sought help for their neighbor, who refused to leave her home. Miriam had a lump on her head and a pair of black eyes. Larry, despite being thrown from his crib, was not hurt.[23]

Gladys Geesey took these shots in Delaware County while volunteering for the American Red Cross. (Gladys Geesey)

6

"Did You Say a Church Stood There?"

Lorain County

Of all of Ohio's Palm Sunday tornadoes, it was the only one that weather expert Thomas Grazulus would later identify as an F5, the level at the top of the Fujita Scale of tornado intensity. F5's make up one-tenth of one percent of all tornadoes, yet they account for nearly twenty-four percent of tornado deaths. The damage from an F5 tornado is described as "Incredible," and anyone who survived the monster twister that struck Lorain and Cuyahoga Counties on April 11, 1965, would readily agree.[1]

Among the first people to experience one of the most destructive tornadoes in Ohio's history were Charles and Linda Knapp and their children, Sherry, David, and Bonny. The Knapps lived on Whitney Road in Pittsfield Township, Lorain County. Pittsfield Township is located between the city of Oberlin and the village of Wellington. Then as now, the tiny village of Pittsfield, or Pittsfield Center, was the largest community in the township. The Knapps lived one and one-half miles southwest of the village.

The farm family had worked hard that day and gone to bed early. Sherry (Knapp) Norton recalls being awakened by a noise "like someone took all the cupboards and dumped everything on the floor." Bonny was in the same room, Sherry recalls, "and we were screaming, not knowing what was going on." Linda remembers being "awakened by a tremendous noise." She heard a board hit a window and got up, but the pressure would not allow her to open the bedroom door until the tornado had passed. David slept through the storm. As for Charles, "When I heard the glass [breaking]," he says, "I just pulled the covers over myself." However, he got up in time to witness a funnel "three hundred to four hundred feet wide at the top. It was huge," he continues, "and you could hear the roar off in the distance, like a jet."

Three barns on an adjoining farm, some 250 feet from the Knapp house, were destroyed. Their debris broke windows and damaged siding on the Knapp home. "There was stuff flying everywhere," Linda says, and she ended up with several cuts from debris that entered the house. A large tree from their yard blocked the road, and Charles's pickup truck was blown 200 feet away and blasted by debris. It is possible, Charles adds, that two tornadoes converged beyond the Knapp home. He recalls two separate damage paths, one about fifty feet wide, the other three times that width.[2]

A short distance northeast of the Knapp home, on Pitts Road, just west of Pittsfield, the roaring funnel awoke Dave Nash. He got out of bed, planning to alert his wife, Gerry, and daughters Cathy and Kim. He never got to.

Suddenly the tornado lifted him over a dresser and sent him flying through the house. It flung him through the living room window and outside, where he could see large balls of fire from high tension lines. Nash was afraid he would fly into them. "I was grasping for anything I could get hold of," he says, but there was nothing to grab. He landed in the driveway, northwest of his original position, some eighty-five feet from the house. He did not hit anything, nor did he land particularly hard. "I just stopped," he recalls. The sky was solid with lightning, "like an arc welder. I looked up," he continues, "and the house was gone, exploded like a bomb had hit the house."

Nash yelled for his wife and "heard her rattling around." Gerry had been watching television-- Bonanza, of course-- in another bedroom and had fallen asleep during the news. She awoke still in bed, but the bed had been moved. Debris and rafters were all around, and a two-by-four and a partial wall were atop her. Above were the sky and lightning. Dave uncovered her, then they heard Kim crying. She was in the back yard, her thigh severely cut. Most likely her bed had hit a tree and one of the many pieces of bathroom fixtures lying around had cut her. Their other daughter had wandered into the garage area. Cathy (Nash) Bowman remembers hearing the tornado, but the family lived adjacent to a railroad track, and she assumed it was a train. "I heard a noise, and then it was gone," she says. Her next memory is of pushing lumber off her body.

Dave managed to drive his car to State Route 58, but heavy rain and a broken windshield made it impossible to continue. They returned to their driveway. Two cars passed by before a pair of men heading to work took the family to the Wellington Hospital. Kim was later transferred to Elyria. The scene at the hospital, Nash says, was "chaos." He was cut all over but most severely on his head and ankles. It took some one hundred stitches to patch him up. "He's held together by string," a physician at the hospital told the *Elyria Chronicle-Telegram*. Someone told Nash he looked as if he had "gone through a meat grinder." With unintended irony the doctor told the paper, "He's not seriously hurt, but cut to pieces."

Relatives guarded the Nash home site from looters, who arrived soon after the storm passed through, but there was nothing left to guard. Dave's father found Gerry's purse and a little money, but that was about it. The family dog was found dead by the railroad tracks. As bad as he was hurt, Dave's decision to get up when he did may have saved him from more serious injury or death. His mattress was in the top of a tree.[3]

Just south of Pittsfield, Anne Broud watched as a severe electrical storm passed through. Worried about the lights going off, she got the kerosene lamps out. As she did, "I heard this fearful roar," Mrs. Broud recalls. She assumed it was a train or an airplane. It was not until the next morning that she heard the news on the radio. Her daughter, who lived in Lakewood, also heard about the storm. Rushing to her parents' home, she was stopped in Pittsfield by the police. She was not even aware that she had reached Pittsfield. "She couldn't even recognize it," Mrs. Broud points out.[4]

That was because there was virtually nothing left of Pittsfield Center to recognize. The hamlet had taken a direct hit from a ferocious F5 tornado, and as one rescue worker told a reporter, "The whole town's gone." That included fourteen houses, two churches, three businesses, and numerous barns and outbuildings "flattened or seriously damaged," the *Wellington Enterprise* reported. "The entire center of Pittsfield was a shambles," the paper continued. *Lorain Journal* society editor Lou Kepler, a Pittsfield native, wrote in the *Enterprise*, "Tears rolled down my cheeks as I looked where my church, the Pittsfield Methodist Church, stood. In the debris," Kepler continued, "was a tattered American flag that stood next to the pulpit. The brass urn that was on the altar rested on a portion of the fallen roof." Hymnals were scattered everywhere, one opened to the hymn, "God Bless This House." Pittsfield's other church, the Congregational Church, "was reduced to a mass of twisted roof, splintered pews and broken beams. A pile of bricks next to it," Kepler wrote, "was the town hall." Mixed in were the remains of the community's grocery store and gas station. About the only object that was recognizable was the community's Civil War monument, but even it was not unscathed. The stone soldier who had stood vigil atop it lay on the ground close by.[5]

The damage astounded Ohio Governor James A. Rhodes, who visited Pittsfield the next day as he toured Ohio's storm-struck communities. At one point the governor asked a reporter, "Did you say a church stood there?" He then said, "This is terrible."[6]

Nine people died in or close to Pittsfield Center. Two were residents of Lorain, who were passing through in separate vehicles. Oberlin funeral director Garnard Cowling was among the first people to reach the community after the storm hit. He told the *Lorain Journal* there was "no sound, no lights, no life, not anybody" when he arrived. "Except for the wind and the rain there was no motion," Cowling said. "It was a desolate area." Finally he met two young men with flashlights, who directed him to where the two motorists lay. One, a woman, was dead in a ditch. The other, a man, was in the road. He was still alive, but he later died at the Elyria Memorial Hospital.[7]

The other deaths included three members of one family. Richard "Dick" Dewey and two of his children, Sandra, age four, and Stephen, age six months, died when the tornado destroyed their home. East of Pittsfield Center Prof. Addison Ward, an assistant professor of English at Oberlin College, died, along with his eight-year old son, Peter. Also killed at Pittsfield were Louis Klier, who owned the community's grocery store, and Mrs. Eva Robey. Mrs. Robey lived at the home of her son. The son, along with his wife and his two sons, survived when their house exploded and fell atop them. He later told a reporter, "The only thing [we] did among that wreckage was pray."[8]

Among the destruction were remarkable stories of survival. One of the most remarkable was that of Rev. Elmer Novak and his family. Rev. Novak was a student at the Oberlin College Graduate School of Theology and was serving the Pittsfield Congregational Church as pastor. He and his wife, Ruth, lived in the parsonage with daughter Bethany (Stipp), then five years old, and son Benjamin, who was eight months old. The parsonage was on Route 303 west of Route 58. The church was next door to the east, and east of that was the park, where Pittsfield's Civil War monument still stands.

The couple went to bed about 11:00 p.m., knowing, Rev. Novak recalls, "we were on the eastern edge of the warning area." They had fallen asleep, but were jolted awake by something. "We don't know what woke us up," Rev. Novak says. "Suddenly we were out of bed running for the children." Elmer headed for his daughter's bedroom and got Bethany as Ruth lifted Ben from his crib. Ruth recalls the sight of bushes pressed flat against a window and "hearing strange noises, a constant roar." They got to the kitchen, on their way to the basement, when "the house started vibrating," Rev. Novak says. There was no conversation, he adds, but "just instinctively" they dived under the kitchen table and covered the children as glass started breaking. Debris pelted them, the pastor notes, "like being in a sand blast. The next thing I know," he continues, "I woke up in the park."

"The floor came up and hit you in the face," Ruth says of the moment of impact, and, "the kids weren't there." The only member of the family who remained conscious, she recalls being dragged, her hands outstretched trying to grasp anything she could. She felt gravel, likely from the driveway, and remembers being "tossed around a little bit and dumped in the field in mud," thankfully soft. She lay there for several seconds, not sure she was alive. She could see lightning, but could not hear the thunder. Through one flash she saw Bethany and grabbed her. "What happened?" she asked. "It was something like The Wizard of Oz," her mother replied. Another flash, and there was Ben, draped over a cinder block, unconscious. She picked him up, and he soon came to. Ruth stood up, trying to orient herself as lightning flashes illuminated the scene. She saw Elmer, standing, looking through the lightning too, and yelled for him.

Together they tried to decide which way to go. "We didn't know where we were exactly," Rev. Novak says. Their only reference point was the Civil War monument, and they began walking west from it. As they did they heard a young woman call for help. It was the daughter of Louis Klier, one of Pittsfield's fatalities. "It was one of the worst moments of my life," Rev. Novak relates, knowing he could do nothing to assist her. They walked, Ruth says, until they came "to this big hole," which they decided was the church basement. Folding chairs from the church were all around, and being barefoot, they tried to walk on them.

They walked toward lights on Route 58. The lights belonged to motorists who had arrived after the storm hit to see if they could help. "They were very nice people," Ruth says. "We were blood and mud," Elmer adds, but a man nevertheless drove them to the Oberlin Hospital. It was, Rev. Novak jokes, "my first experience with streaking." He was wearing nothing but the elastic band of his shorts. As they headed north, it began to hail, and Ruth remembers thinking, "If it didn't get us the first time, it's going to get us the second."

It didn't. They entered the hospital, Elmer in a wheelchair, Ruth walking. She got through the door and sat down in the corridor, able to go no further. She regained her strength, however, and walked to the emergency room. There she held her composure long enough to provide names, ages, and allergy information to hospital workers. Eventually the adrenalin or the immediate emotion or something else wore off. "And then," Ruth says, "I think you realize how much you hurt." She had no broken bones, but, "I didn't have much area that didn't have a big black and blue mark on it." Her husband adds, "We looked like somebody took a baseball bat to us." The entire family remained in the hospital for a week.

The Novaks returned to a parsonage that was nothing more than a foundation. They never saw their appliances. Indeed, the only thing identifiable from the main floor of their home was a window frame. The water heater and the furnace had been tossed around in the basement. The wind removed the huge cement cover of their cistern. The congregation rented a house for them and completely furnished it, even putting food in the cupboards. Ruth had "nightmares for probably three years" after her ordeal; and to this day, she adds, "We head for the basement when there are storm warnings."[9]

Another miraculous Pittsfield Center survivor was eighty-one-year old Clayton Pickworth. According to his grandson, Robert Diedrick, Pickworth later related that he got out of bed to put on his pants "and the damn west wall came in on me." He got up, tried again, "and the damn east wall came in on me." The next thing Mr. Pickworth remembered was waking up in a field five hundred feet from his house. Pieces of fiberglass were embedded in his skin. His home was destroyed. Indeed, says Clayton's son, Paul O. Pickworth, Pittsfield Center was "just like kindling." His father remained in the hospital for a week,

Pickworth says. Very little of his property could be recovered, but students from Oberlin College retrieved his pocketbook with all the money still in it.[10]

At least one survival story dated back to sixteen years before. In 1949 Warren and Helen Harris, both of whom had been raised on farms, decided to purchase a farm of their own. They were interested in a property along Route 303. However, Helen's mother talked them out of it. According to Caroline M. Harris, the Harrises' daughter, "Grandma persuaded them not to buy because it was 'tornado territory.' Where my grandmother got this information," Caroline says, "is unknown." The woman's warnings were persuasive, and the Harrises instead purchased a farm on Quarry Road. It was a wise decision, because the home they nearly bought was extensively damaged. Helen seemed to inherit her mother's sixth sense about weather. The morning of the storm, Caroline says, "I recall my mother looked toward the heavens and said, 'There's going to be a tornado tonight.'"

Caroline's aunt, Mrs. Elmer (Lillian) Harris, also lived on Quarry Road. "I never saw lightning so bad," she says of that night. "It was blue flashes." Her home, too, was spared. Her son, David, played an important role in the rescue effort, running gasoline and supplies from Oberlin to Pittsfield.[11]

There were several heroes around Pittsfield that night. One of them was Charles Jackson. "He rescued all the neighbors around him," one woman told the *Elyria Chronicle-Telegram*. An employee of Columbia Gas, Jackson spent much of Palm Sunday helping his brother in Elyria put an addition on his house. He returned to his home on Route 303 and soon after heard the "freight train" sound. He told his wife to get their four girls and head for the basement, but by then, "It was there." Jackson and his family were unhurt, but a thirty-foot section of their house was out in the highway, "as a trucker found out when he came down the road," Jackson adds. He slammed on the brakes but still hit the debris. The trucker was not hurt.

Jackson almost immediately went looking for his neighbors. The first one he found was Clayton Pickworth. "I got my one pant leg on," the octogenarian told him, "then I don't know what happened." Jackson found him with that one leg still on. He then located a woman who was badly cut and took her to the remains of the Jackson home. At about the same time Oberlin police officer Gene Barlow arrived, blocked the road, and began summoning ambulances. After helping retrieve the body of Eva Robey, Jackson says, "We just kept looking and finding people and bringing them to the house." Eventually seventeen ended up there. Most were children, and most had only minor injuries. As Jackson went back out to shut off gas lines, his wife, Barbara, played the piano to try to calm the children. "One by one," he says, "they went to sleep."[12]

82   The Night of the Wicked Winds

The Dave Nash family survived the total destruction of their home, just west of Pittsfield. Note the downed utility pole in the yard. (Dave and Gerry Nash)

Charles Jackson examines the remains of a Pittsfield home. The debris behind is from the Paul Pickworth home. Behind that a new township hall goes up. (Charles Jackson)

Two views of the total destruction in Pittsfield. (Cleveland Public Library)

Also out aiding his neighbors that night-- and recovering their bodies-- was Perry Brandt, who lived on Route 58 a short distance north of the junction with Route 303. Just before 11:00 p.m., Brandt picked up his daughter, Bonnie, who was working at an ice cream drive in a short distance north of his farm. The family went to bed, but Bonnie soon came to her parents' room and told Brandt and his wife, Lois, "I don't like it. It's too quiet." They all then heard the sound of the approaching tornado. The three headed for the basement, along with Lois's mother, Alice Mills, who lived with them, and the Brandts' daughter Nancy. Mrs. Mills wanted to stop and get her new coat, but when the limb of a pine tree came crashing through a window she forgot the coat. The family reached safety and was uninjured, but their house was seriously damaged. The tree caved in the front porch, and half of the roof was gone. There was also a great deal of debris to remove. Groups of Amish, Brandt notes, later arrived to help with the clean-up.

After the storm had passed, Brandt went outside to survey the damage. His neighbor to the south, Carl Dewey, soon came over with his wife, Catherine, who was quite agitated. Catherine stayed at the Brandt home while Perry and Carl went to check on the Deweys' son, Dick, who lived just east of Pittsfield Center. The two men reached the site and discovered that Dick's home was gone. They continued east, through a field and on to a pond. There Perry found Dick and his two girls. Dick and one of his daughters were dead (as was a son, found by others). The other girl was alive, and Brandt carried her to Route 58 and a waiting ambulance. A television news crew was filming as he did. That footage made the national news, and that was how Perry's brother, living in Clemson, South Carolina, learned that he had survived the tornado.[13]

For Jean McConnell and her family destruction was less than a mile away. The day, Jean recalls, had been beautiful, but with "a real strange color in the sky" by five in the afternoon. The sky was "pinkish" and everything was still and silent, no birds flying nor dogs barking. Jean and her husband, Howard, lived three-fourths of a mile south of Pittsfield on a farm. It was close enough for them to hear the roar of the twister. They dashed to the basement, where the sound of the wind could be heard "terrifically" through the stone foundation. Damage at the McConnell farm was relatively light. Part of a barn roof was gone, and chunks of debris dotted the fields. Howard and son Mark joined their neighbors in walking the fields looking for victims. They later found a beam from the Congregational Church in the woods a mile away. At Howard's parents' farm, located nearby, fence posts remained in place but flying debris tore out all the fence.[14]

A short distance east of Pittsfield Center on Route 303 was the home of Henry and Amy Sheffield and their son Tom. Another son, Jim, lived about a half mile south of Pittsfield, and he was up watching what he thought was a strong thunderstorm. That was until a visitor arrived to tell him what had happened at Pittsfield. Sheffield hurried to his parents' home, which was no longer there. All three occupants, he would later learn, had started for the basement but had not made it. He found his mother in a ditch beneath some rubble. "You're walking on top of me," she said. Mrs. Sheffield also told Jim that his father had gone for help. Henry had a severe cut across his throat. In seeking assistance he frightened the occupants of one car, who turned and sped away. Tom had been blown through a window and suffered a broken arm. Mrs. Sheffield had a severed spinal cord. She spent the next four months in the hospital and remained a paraplegic the rest of her life. Impressions of siding in the ground, Sheffield notes, indicated that the house had rolled. Little remained, but a woman from Oberlin spent an entire day picking through a field to return the Sheffields' coin collection. The mailbox was found four miles away. To this day, Sheffield plows up pieces of debris from the fields.[15]

One mile east of Pittsfield on Route 303 Robert Diedrick and his six brothers and sisters were in bed. His parents, Robert J. and Betty, had been in bed but could not sleep. They got up and heard television weatherman Dick Goddard tell about a tornado in Toledo. Then the power went out. The Diedricks went to the stairs to summon the children downstairs. By then windows were breaking, but no one in the house was seriously hurt, nor did the house sustain serious damage. The rest of the farm did not fare as well. As the tornado blew by, Mr. Diedrick looked out the window and saw a silo roof suspended in the air. The storm lifted the wooden upper half of their barn into the air and sent it crashing down as it blew in the cement block lower section. Some thirty-five of the forty-three cattle in the barn were killed. All other farm buildings, including an eighty-foot steel tool shed, were destroyed as well.[16]

"We heard it coming; we heard the roar," says Phyllis Langdon, who lived with her husband, Howard, and their son, Kenneth, on Hawley Road, a mile and a half northeast of Pittsfield. All three ran for the basement. Halfway down the stairs, dirt and slag peppered them. The tornado had lifted their house from its foundation and blown in driveway slag. It removed the east side of the dwelling, including the kitchen and the dining room. Their car came down on a workbench. Prof. Ward's home was located across the road. "It all went down," Phyllis remembers. The Wards' son had been camping out in the barn and was uninjured. He came to the Langdons' door and said, "My house is down, and I think my folks are dead." Howard and a neighbor, Ray Bradley, went over. The boy's mother, although trapped in the basement, survived. Bradley used his chain saw to cut a beam under which she was lodged. As noted above, the Wards' other son, Peter, died.[17]

Scene at the Robert J. Diedrick farm east of Pittsfield. (Robert Diedrick)

To the north, on Hughes Road, Donna (Widdowson) Sears was troubled by the approaching storm. "It was just something about the way the lightning was," she says. It bothered her enough that she herded her six children behind a stairwell. Their home did not have a basement, but she felt a cement wall behind the stairwell would provide protection. "They didn't like it," she recalls, but the young mother was adamant. Donna heard an abnormal sound above the youngsters' chatter, but the tornado missed them. After the storm seemed past, she put the kids to bed. Then, looking out her bedroom window south, Donna noticed that she could view traffic on Route 303 without any breaks. Normally homes and barns blocked the view in several places. She and her husband drove south and beheld scenes of destruction. At one farm a couple was looking for a missing boy. He was later found, still wrapped in his covers, asleep and unhurt, beneath a section of roof.[18]

The Wendell F. Cotton family also lived on Hughes Road, although they had excavated to build a new house near the residence of Professor Ward. News of tornadoes in Illinois and Indiana, along with "bumpy, rough looking clouds," Cotton recalls, alarmed the family. "We were all kind of nervous," he says, "and could not sleep." Nervousness turned to fright when the Cottons heard a "tremendous roar like a herd of elephants." Cotton and his wife, Marie F., got their four children and put them under two couches in the living room.

Workers clean up the Pittsfield Park. (Cleveland Public Library)

The four Cotton children, all interviewed separately, have similar memories of that night. Ryan remembers his father summoning him from his sleep to go downstairs and his mother putting the living room couches in a circular formation. (The home had no basement.) Mrs. Cotton told the kids to get between them and put the cushions over their heads. The lights went out, he heard the freight train sound, and the large picture window vibrated but did not break. Tyler, at age five the youngest, recalls the "abrupt nature of my parents stuffing us under furniture" and "machine gun fire against the window" as debris struck it. Brad also remembers hearing things hitting the house, plus a "real roaring sound." Corinne (Cotton) Precourt, the only Cotton girl, may have been the boldest. She heard the freight train roar but still summoned the courage to peak from the family's improvised shelter. Through the window she saw a "gray, churning funnel."

After the tornado had passed, Mr. Cotton looked out the front door, which faced east, for his own view of the funnel. The kids followed, looking out an east window. "We were just in awe," Ryan says. "This thing was like an elephant compared to the wispy things you see in pictures." Based on the road grid, he placed its width at one-half mile. To Brad, viewing it through "continuous lightning," it appeared to be "a mile-wide column."

Acting against his wife's wishes, Wendell went out to see if he could help anyone. Debris, including the Sheffield house on Route 303, blocked his way at several locations. The Ward home, a three-story brick house, was leveled, he recalls. Yet some knickknacks from a curio cabinet were not touched. Several beams struck Professor Ward, killing him. His glasses, however, were not broken.

The Cotton family awoke the next morning to a scene of devastation-- and traffic. There were, Tyler says, "monumental long lines of cars." Corinne remembers wondering, "Why are all these people coming?" The sight of a huge barn beam in their yard brought a sobering point home to both Ryan and Tyler. It had come from the Ward barn, three-fourths of a mile away, and had missed their picture window by only a few feet. Aluminum from silos garnished the yard. "It looked like somebody had come down with a mile-wide hand," Brad says, and he was left with an "overwhelming feeling of awe." When Corinne went out she had "this sinking feeling of, 'My, there used to be a house there.'" An essay she later wrote as a school assignment helped her work through the trauma of what she saw. Still, she remembers heading for the cellar of their new home whenever she heard any weather warnings. Ryan, too, says tornado watches made him nervous after what he had experienced. Brad feels the tornado and its aftermath may have helped influence his decision to become a volunteer fireman as well as his career choice. He is an emergency room physician in Chillicothe. For Tyler the events of April 11, 1965, inspired a lifelong interest in weather. "It's always been rabid," he says of the obsession. He is active in his local meteorological society and has made storm chasing trips to Oklahoma, although he is yet to experience his second tornado.[19]

Norma Roberts normally worked two or three nights a week as a nurse's aid at Southern Lorain County Hospital, a twenty-eight-bed facility in Wellington. Having worked the night before, she had no way of knowing Sunday evening that she was about to begin the most intense night of her career, a shift that would not end until seven or eight the next morning. She and her husband, Francis, were watching a movie on television. Meanwhile, their dog kept "fussing." Then the lights went off, and the couple moved to the dining room table and watched as a strong storm hit. The phone rang. It was her boss calling her to work. "There's been a tornado in Pittsfield," he said, "and it's bad."

The Night of the Wicked Winds 89

An employee of the Lorain Metropolitan Park Commission treats the wounds on the soldier from Pittsfield's Civil War monument. (Cleveland Public Library)

"The people just started coming in," she says. Ambulatory patients already there were moved to a big meeting room in the basement to make room for tornado victims. "Before the night was over," she says, "there were patients up and down both halls" of the one-story hospital. The lobby, too, was eventually full. The countenances of the patients "was just like disbelief. I can't remember anybody being the slightest bit hysterical." One woman, asked her marital status, answered, "Widowed." Asked when she had become a widow, the woman replied, "Tonight."[20]

Another Wellington resident, Dorothy (Nutter) George, did not even know the tornado had hit a few miles to the north. To her it was simply a strong wind storm that had blown down her yard light. The next morning she headed north to Allen Memorial Hospital in Oberlin, where her husband was a cancer patient. Upon reaching Pittsfield, she beheld dead cattle, clothes hanging from trees, and a farm house across the road from where it had been. She had to take a detour to reach Oberlin. The injured still crowded the hospital when she got there. Among them, she recalls, was a woman who "had splinters all over her."[21]

"Pittsfield aims to stay on map." That headline in the *Oberlin News-Tribune* summed up succinctly the attitude of a devastated but determined community. Elyria businessman Samuel B. Katz loaned the township a forty-by-sixty-foot inflatable building, which went up in the park. It became the headquarters for the clean-up and rebuilding effort. On the sixteenth, a Pittsfield Township trustee told the *Lorain Journal*, "We are making progress and we are certainly grateful to the hundreds here to help us." Those helpers included some fifty boys from Wellington High School, who cleaned rubble from the Pittsfield Cemetery and searched for numerous missing gravestones. The Wellington contingent later included a number of girls, upset when they were not included in their school's initial call for volunteers. Dozens of Oberlin College students also helped. "I have never seen anything like this," one man said. "These college kids are great." The Lorain Metropolitan Park Commission repaired Pittsfield's wounded stone sentry and placed him back atop the Civil War monument. Other volunteers ranged from Boy Scouts and Oberlin High School students to inmates from the Lorain County jail.[22]

Pittsfield's Methodist Church had stood since 1845, the Congregational Church since 1849. Both congregations dated back even farther. Despite those long histories, the two churches decided to merge in the wake of the tornado. They gathered the following Sunday at an old Assembly of God church building north of town. Frank N. Evard, lay pastor of the Methodist Church, conducted the service. Rev. Novak, just released from the hospital, attended. Evard spoke of a Pittsfield with "a future far greater than its past." He told those assembled, "We will build a new town center, one united church, serving the people of the community, bearing a strong witness to the saving power of Jesus Christ." According to Rev. Novak, the rebuilding process went relatively smoothly. In general, he says, "The people really worked well together." Monetary aid arrived from many denominations. Each congregation, the pastor notes, wanted the new church built on their lot. Instead, it was constructed at the southwest corner of Routes 303 and 58, where the Pittsfield Community Church still serves an active congregation.[23]

The next community in the storm's path, a short distance east of Pittsfield, was Lagrange. There six people died as the tornado hit the northern edge of the community. Among them were Bruce and Elsie Gibbons, whose tragedy was laced with irony. The couple had been preparing for a trip to Florida, a prize they had won the previous Christmas. They planned to leave the next day. Forty-one years earlier, Bruce had served with the Ohio National Guard. He was among those assigned to duty when a deadly tornado struck Lorain in 1924. His future wife, then Elsie Biro, had been at Lorain's Lakeview Park that day with two friends. The three girls had left just fifteen minutes before that twister roared in off Lake Erie. The Gibbons home was "flattened," according to the *Wellington Enterprise*, as was the home of their neighbor, Leon Speake, who also died. A short distance east, on Wheeler Road, the twister blew James C. Wilson and his eight-month old son 700 feet from their home, killing them both. Wilson's wife and daughter were critically injured.[24]

Ed Burke, who lived with his parents a short distance west of Lagrange on Diagonal Road, had spent much of Palm Sunday riding his new motorcycle. By the time he returned home at about 8:30 that evening it had grown very calm. He watched television for a while, then went to bed at about ten. Dozing, he saw lightning and heard thunder, which grew more intense. The wind had returned when his mother ran upstairs and shouted, "Get up! We're having a tornado." By the time he got down to the main floor of the house, Burke heard a roar that led him to believe a jet was crashing. He got three steps down to the basement when all the windows started breaking. The ceiling lifted, and "you could look up and see the sky." The wind had taken the house off its foundation. As debris came crashing down, Burke had trouble breathing. "It was like it was sucking the air right out of you," he recalls.

Although his last memory was of being in the basement, Burke suddenly found himself standing in the yard. Through the lightning he saw the main funnel plus a second funnel cloud, which scared him more than what he had just been through. Looking back toward the house he saw a flashlight beam. His mother was holding the flashlight. The washing machine was next to her. Then he saw his father with sandstone atop him. Burke assumed he was dead until he heard him groan. He managed to extricate his father, and with his mother's help, took him toward the home of his neighbors, Joe and Rosemary Zalka. Another neighbor drove by and took all three to the hospital in Oberlin. There Burke remembers watching as Pittsfield residents, many horribly injured, were brought in. He was bruised, but his parents were more badly hurt. A piece of sandstone had hit his mother, leaving her with a concussion that kept her in the hospital for five days. His father remained hospitalized for about ten days. He had broken several ribs right at the spinal cord. His injuries led to permanent back problems.

Burke's sister, Linda, picked him up the next morning. "I've been out to the farm," she said, "and you're not going to recognize it." Even that warning could not prepare him for the sight that greeted him upon his return home. Nothing was left of the house, nor of the barn, the granary, a detached garage, and the chicken coop. The legs of dead cattle stuck out from the remains of the barn. The car had rolled end over end for about a fourth of a mile. One farm wagon was never found. Nothing was left from inside the house, including the family's clothes, with the exception of an antique spinning wheel, which was virtually undamaged. Corn covered Burke's motorcycle, protecting it from serious damage. Planks driven into the ground dotted a rise to the east. "It looked like boot hill," Burke says.[25]

For Burke's neighbors, the Zalkas, the story had a similar beginning. Kathy Zalka was in bed when she heard her mother shouting for her and her two sisters to hurry downstairs. "This sounds like a tornado," she recalls Mrs. Zalka saying, to which her father replied, "It is. Get the kids." Kathy and her sister Rosemary dashed down the stairs. The third sister, Martha, remained upstairs. Waking up to rain coming in and plaster falling down, "I covered up my head and went back to sleep," Martha says. With her father holding her, Rosemary remembers the suction of the storm strongly pulling her back up the stairs. The tornado unroofed their home and flattened two barns and their garage. Some seven cattle were killed.[26]

The tornado produced severe damage just north of Lagrange along Route 301. One of the homes hit was a farm house that had been home for six months to Marla (Gott) Koviak and her husband. The Gotts' first sign of impending trouble came at about 10:45, when their dog began barking "horribly." They brought the dog inside and gathered their five children, including three infants. "We didn't hear a thing until it hit," Marla says. She covered three of the children, later finding a soda bottle embedded in a wall where she had been standing. The wind blew her husband through the house until he caught onto one of the beds. One of the babies and the Gotts' ten-year old son, Duane, were missing but quickly found, alive and well. The north wall of their house was gone, and everything from the exposed rooms was lying across the road in a field. Spears of glass glistened from the crib of their twin babies. Seven trees were down in the front yard, pieces of straw sticking out of them. Mr. Gott's semi truck had been thrown thirty feet until the house stopped it. A shed ended up in the kitchen, and glass ended up in the freezer. They found a Pittsfield village limits sign in the back yard.

The Gotts went to Marla's mother's home in Elyria. The sight of the family, glass in their hair and superficially embedded in everyone's skin, shocked her. Family members brought in baby clothes, and help appeared from many sources. A passerby found Marla's purse in the front yard and returned it. One man was fired from his carpet laying firm because he missed work to aid the Gotts. At the other end of the spectrum were the individual who stole their bathroom sink and the neighbor who forbade the family from retrieving anything blown onto his property.

Many of the fatalities were Marla's neighbors. The Gibbonses, she recalls, were found in a field "riddled with glass." Leon Speake, she says, died en route to the hospital. He had refused to be moved until he received assurance that all the Gott children were safe. They were, but the babies' noses, Marla adds, ran black afterward from dirty insulation.

Their home could not be repaired, and the Gotts sold the property. The experience, Marla notes, changed her priorities, making her more compassionate toward others. She worked for twenty-nine years after as a nurse. She concludes, "You look at things in a different light."[27]

Marvin and Ellie Marsh had bought their home on Route 301 the previous November. Marvin was an air traffic controller, working at Oberlin for Cleveland-Hopkins Airport. He was scheduled to leave for work at 11:15.

He didn't. Ellie recalls that her husband suddenly awakened her and said a bad storm was coming. She grabbed their young sons, Gregory and Douglas, and headed for the basement. Marvin had told her to take some food, so she also had a five-pound can of potato chips. The couple watched as the funnel approached from the west. As it neared, Ellie lay over the boys. She heard "a whooshing noise" and things breaking above. Then it was over. Marvin went to check on their neighbors, returning with instructions to Ellie to get some blankets. The house was badly damaged but repairable. A barn door had crashed through the living room wall. Their car ended up in the Gibbonses' basement, and Marvin's boat was a half mile away in a tree. Items from the basement were in the living room, and vice versa. The Marshes removed a bushel of glass from their bed, and they too had a Pittsfield sign. They found it between their mattress and box spring.[28]

John Poulton and his brother Rodney slept downstairs that night. Their mother, worried by the storm warnings, had insisted. At 11:25, his brother recalls, Rodney said, "Hey Johnny, take a look at this." Their windows were bowing in and out, but they did not break. Outside the boys saw flashes and fireballs from high tension lines. They went to school the next morning. All the students were taken into the auditorium and told that classes were cancelled. "That's the first we'd heard of it," John says. School officials asked for volunteers to search for victims and help clean up. Both John, a fourth grader, and Rodney, who was in the sixth grade, stepped forward, got in buses, and headed north of town. The students were paired with adults. They spent the day gathering wood, glass, and other debris. Boats were wrapped in trees, and cars sat in the woods. One high tension mast was "twisted like you wadded up paper." The most unusual thing Poulton saw was a cow in a tree. The students received pillow cases to collect personal effects, which the chief of police took to an announced area for people to claim. The boys worked for three or four days. "We saw anything that you'd see in a house," Poulton says. "It just looked like one big landfill."[29]

Another youthful volunteer was Jim Seabold. The Seabolds heard the tornado coming and went to the basement. They emerged to find their home not seriously damaged. Their neighbors' house was gone. Helping in the clean-up effort, Seabold says, his group located "a lot of barns and buildings we knew from the area were gone." Judi Buga, a student at Keystone High School, recalls being at the scene when injured cattle were shot. Pictures, plates, and similar personal items stand out in her memory of the debris. Some glass items, she says, survived unharmed. So did a pet rabbit belonging to one of her friends. Its hutch was destroyed, but the family found the bunny two days later, unhurt but still shaking. The tornado did not hit the Buga home, located on Indian Hollow Road, but they heard it. Judi's mother, Mrs. Frank Buga, Sr. (Emily), recalls, "It just roared and roared."[30]

From Lagrange the tornado roared northeast into Grafton, where it damaged nearly three hundred homes. Mayor Maurice Bittner told reporters that at least 150 of them had what he described as "medium to serious damage." Especially hard hit was a neighborhood including Hickory, Willow, and Mechanic Streets, where approximately thirty houses were hit, many destroyed or beyond repair. The village park lost two-thirds of its trees. One Grafton resident, a high school student, told the *Elyria Chronicle-Telegram* that she ran from her bedroom to her mother's room when a pair of lightning strikes frightened her. "It's a good thing I did," the girl added, "because I'd be dead now. A bath tub landed on top of my bed." In another case a small boy ran from his bedroom just before "a huge rock" crashed through the window and landed on the bed. Among the most relieved people, Mrs. Elmer (Lillian) Harris recalls, was a group of students on a senior trip to New York. Her daughter, Martha (Harris) Pendleton, was chaperoning the group. When they heard about the tornado on television they became frantic with worry, trying without success to call home. It was some time before they learned that their families were all well. One man was not so lucky. He became Lorain County's eighteenth fatality when he died two days after the storm struck.[31]

"Grafton was a mess," recalls Robert Meyer, who worked for the Lorain County engineer's office. "I just couldn't believe all the destruction." Meyer was a mechanic, normally working at the garage, but in an emergency, "We all had to do everything." He was called out at 6:00 a.m. on Monday. His crew went first to Pittsfield, where the scene "looked like somebody dropped a bomb." At Grafton there were "people and junk all over the place." One home, he remembers, was completely gone, with the exception of one bedroom. The ceiling of the room was gone, but all four walls were intact, and the occupant had slept through the storm unhurt. He also saw a number of looters. "They were always in the way," Meyer says, "and the sheriff's deputies couldn't keep them out of the way." Meyer adds, "I couldn't believe that people would be that callous."[32]

Among Grafton's survivors were D. John and Ruth Grobske and their five children. The family had gone to bed about 10:30. "My husband heard the noise first," Ruth recalls, "roaring like a freight train." He said, "That's wind. Get the kids to the basement." They did not make it, however. The tornado struck their home as they raced to the basement, and "in about fifteen seconds the whole thing had gone through." The interior of their home was filled with glass, and there was a great deal of exterior damage. Two-by-fours had been driven into closets, and shingles from a neighbor's house were stuck in their living room wall. Their garage and breezeway were gone, resting in the basement of a house on Hickory Street the storm had destroyed. Despite the damage, the Grobske home was the last one on their section of Willow Street that could be repaired. According to Mrs. Grobske, Grafton may well have had a second tornado victim. An elderly man died less than a month later, she recalls, and neighbors believed his death was related to the shock caused by the storm.[33]

There had been storm predictions on the eleven o'clock news, recalls Bernadine Kubuski, who lived on Sunshine Court. She informed her husband, Ed, who was asleep in the front room, closed the windows, and after observing green lightning, went to get their three children. Then, Bernadine says, "all of a sudden it hit." She rolled daughter Margie under her bed as the bathroom door blew around the hallway. Ed threw himself over their son, Tom, and was struck in the shoulder by a beam from a neighbor's barn. Both Nancy (Kubuski) Caithaml and her sister, Margie (Kubuski) Toombs, recall that the roof was gone by the time they headed for the basement.

After the storm passed, Ed yelled from the basement windows to check on his sister, who lived next door. A doctor had recently treated his vocal chords and instructed him to rest his voice, but Mr. Kubuski shouted through one window at a time until he learned that she was well. At one point, Tom recalls, his father went upstairs. He returned crying and simply said, "It's gone." They never found one piece of shingle or truss from the roof, Tom adds, and the door that had blown down the hall traveled ten feet then made a ninety degree turn. The chimney collapsed into the living room. Yet, Bernadine notes, ornaments and knickknacks on the mantle were untouched. The back of the garage fell intact onto the family's car.

During the night, Ed took the children, one at a time, to his sister's home. Each trip he gingerly stepped over what he believed was an electrical wire. Daylight revealed it to be a kite string. It also revealed unbelievable destruction. "One of the biggest shocks," Bernadine says, "was getting up the next morning, looking out, and seeing the drapes hanging out over the house." For Margie, viewing the scene through a child's eyes, the most unbelievable sight was her swing set. To her it was "the strongest thing in the world," and it was blown down. The Kubuskis were able to salvage a number of personal items, but much was lost either by wind or rain. Their house could not be rebuilt. The family lived with Ed's father, also a Grafton resident, for the remainder of the school year. Later that summer they moved to Elyria.

Scenes of the damage at Grafton. (Robert Meyer)

The Ed Kubuski home in Grafton *after* the clean-up began. (Bernadine Kubuski)

Ed was a teacher and coach at Midview High School, and many students and colleagues helped with the clean-up. Other coaches stored things for the family at their homes. School officials let him use his driver education car for personal transportation. There were monetary donations as well. The Kubuskis rebuilt their lives, but the tornado remains a reference point for them, especially if they can not find something. "Everything in our lives," Nancy says, "is in terms of before or after the tornado."[34]

A short distance east of Grafton, Jeff Wagamon, who was thirteen years old, lived with his parents, J. C. and Beatrice, on Cowley Road. His father's diary entry for April 11 closed, "This is the worst electrical storm I've ever seen. Bed 11:20." Their wall clock stopped at 11:22.

A lightning bolt awakened Beatrice and brought her to the kitchen. She looked out a north window as her husband looked west. Mrs. Wagamon watched as the outside gas light blew over. Then a fifty-five-gallon hog watering barrel from the barn struck the house. The couple huddled in a corner. J. C., still in his farmer's bibs, sheltered Beatrice, who was in her night clothes. Meanwhile Jeff, sleeping upstairs, awoke to the sound of breaking glass. He jumped out of bed and was "peppered with glass and debris. I didn't know what to do," he adds, so he ran back to bed and stuck his head under the pillow. A lull in the storm allowed him to hear his parents shouting for him. Both had feared that the top of the house was gone, Jeff with it, and his mother cut her foot from glass as she ran to find him. "Let's go to the basement," Mr. Wagamon said. "We've been wiped out outside. There's nothing left."

J. C. was a member of the Eaton Township Volunteer Fire Department. With his cars under a barn, he walked a mile to summon help. Jeff spent much of the night at a neighboring farm, using a chain saw to cut dairy cattle out of a barn. With the help of fire department members, he saved a few.

Destruction at the Wagamon farm was extensive. Every window in the house was broken, and much of the roof was gone. A barn and several outbuildings were leveled. A rafter from the granary went through the outside wall of the house and crashed through both the attic and the kitchen ceiling before coming to rest in the kitchen. Manure from the chicken house littered the home, even making its way into kitchen cupboards. A skillet lid went from the kitchen into an upstairs bedroom. Dead rabbits littered the field. Sixty-seven dead sheep lay in a neighbor's field. The Wagamons raised sheep, but all of them were accounted for. No neighboring farmers raised sheep, and the point of origin of the dead flock remained a mystery. One animal story had a happy ending. During the storm Jeff's father saw his chicken coop, where the family's two beagles were, four feet off the ground. They later called for the dogs, but they could not be found. They returned forty-five minutes later, unhurt and "wagging their tails."[35]

The last community hit in Lorain County was Columbia Station, a village on the Cuyahoga County border. A father and infant daughter were killed there, as was a woman who lived a mile away on State Route 82.

Bill Heidinger recalls that it was about 11:17 when he heard something that "sounded like somebody threw a brick through the front window." He got out of bed to discover that most of the windows had been blown out of his home. Some shingles were missing, and his attached garage was twisted off its foundation. No one in his family was injured, but his three-year old daughter's crib had been thrown against a wall. The community's two deaths occurred two houses away. The home, Heidinger says, was "wiped out completely." He had visited with his neighbor earlier that evening. "They just looted everything over there," Heidinger adds, even stripping the dead man's car, which had been thrown into a field.

Heidinger's son, Craig, remembers the sight of the garage, with its panels blown out and only the beams remaining. Glass, he adds, blew across his parents' bedroom, passing above them and sticking in a wall. The family dog, Pepper, had been outside, attached to his dog house with a choker chain. After the storm, dog, chain, and house were gone. Pepper returned a few days later, however. He was hoarse, Craig says, but otherwise unhurt.[36]

Cuyahoga County

Crossing into Cuyahoga County, the tornado attacked the northern portion of Strongsville before lifting. It destroyed eighteen homes, including nine on Carlyle Road, and damaged several others. The storm also struck the St. Joseph Roman Catholic School on Pearl Road. Diocese officials set the damage at "hundreds of thousands of dollars." The wind ripped off a portion of the roof, depositing it in classrooms, and blew out several walls. In its waning moments, the tornado also produced one more fatality, a six-week old girl. The injured crowded Southwest Community Hospital in Berea. [37]

Dorothy Klotzsche remembers hearing the tornado forecast on the radio as she, her husband, Richard, and their seven children returned home from evening church services in Cleveland. Arriving at their home on Richards Drive, the three youngest children and Richard, who had to get up at 3:00 a.m. for work, went to bed. Dorothy and the rest of the family watched a movie on television. It began to rain, followed by hail. As Dorothy went to awaken her husband she "heard this roaring noise like a big jet airplane." She opened the bedroom door just in time to see a window frame come loose and plaster begin falling. Dorothy ran back down the hall to see if any of the children were hurt. One daughter was struck by dishes that were blown out of a kitchen cupboard. Falling plaster hit one of the boys. Neither was badly injured.

Dorothy went to check on a neighbor woman who had been at home with her children. She learned that they had been taken to the hospital. Then she and Richard piled the kids into their ten-passenger station wagon. Some stayed with neighbors, others with Richard's parents in Middleburg Heights. Their house was badly damaged. The roof had hit a neighbor's home, knocking it off the foundation. Despite the damage, they were able to rebuild. The Klotzches returned a fur coat they found against the house. They kept a coal shovel that they discovered on a bed.[38]

Seven-year old Alvin Van Bumble, who lived with his family on Richards Drive, had been sent to bed after watching television. His father stayed up, starting upstairs for bed just as the tornado hit. Suddenly he heard it coming. Glancing to one side he saw a screen door coming toward him. Then a large wooden beam from the cathedral ceiling came down, striking him on the hip. The beam eventually landed across the street. As for Alvin, "The next thing I knew it was pouring down rain." He awoke in the front yard. Bleeding in his stomach would keep him in the hospital for three days. His grandmother, who was living with the family, was only slightly injured. His sister, age two, had a mattress wrapped around her. "She was black and blue from head to toe," Van Bumble says, but not seriously hurt. His mother, he adds, was hospitalized for "a very long period of time." The family's home was leveled. Their car was turned around, and the engine was turned around 180 degrees inside it.[39]

Rusty Taphous was at home that night with his mother, LaVerne, and four brothers and sisters. His father, Harold, was at work. They were sitting in the living room when it began to storm. Things later grew quiet, then "sparks were hitting the window." It was, Taphous believes, small stones being thrown from the road. The family heard "what we thought was a train," and the house shook. They went to the basement.

They returned upstairs to "dead silence throughout the neighborhood." Cousins who had been visiting returned to ask about an alternate route home. There was, they explained, a house blocking the road. About that time a neighbor arrived. He told the Taphouses that a tornado had struck. It skipped over their home, he said, before coming back down to strike St. Joseph's. The family had been lucky. Homes two blocks away were flattened, but their damage consisted of just six missing shingles.[40]

"It was a real eye opener for a freshman in college," says Pat Hoke. A student at Baldwin-Wallace College in Berea and a resident of Lorain County, Pat went with a group from the school that volunteered to assist. She went to Strongsville and helped sort donated clothing. Looking around the neighborhood she was astounded by homes with entire walls and roofs gone but furniture still in place and pictures still hanging on the walls that survived. "People had just nothing," she says. Still, it seemed as if they "had just accepted it." Few were grieving or in shock. "Everyone knew there was a lot of work to be done," Pat says, an attitude which she believes kept them going through such adversity.[41]

The Night of the Wicked Winds 101

A six-week old baby was killed beneath this pile of rubble in Strongsville. (Cleveland Public Library)

Damage at the St. Joseph School in Strongsville. (Cleveland Public Library)

7
Scattered Storms, Scattered Lives

Medina and Summit Counties

Although places such as Toledo and Pittsfield received the bulk of the headlines-- and understandably so-- several other Ohio communities were in the paths of serious tornadoes Palm Sunday night. Among the worst of these less publicized storms was the F3 tornado that cut an eight-mile swath from Brunswick to a point two miles north of Richfield. The twister did its worst damage at Brunswick. Touching down at about 11:30 p.m., it put seven residents of the community in the hospital and left about one hundred people homeless. Among those in both categories was a mother of four whose husband had been killed in an automobile accident just seventeen days before. Continuing into Liverpool Township, the storm demolished two homes and a barn. Six homes in Hinckley were damaged. The greatest financial loss occurred at an automobile dealership where seventy cars, fifty of them new, sustained damage. The owners placed their loss at between $50,000 and $100,000.[1]

One of the hardest hit areas in Brunswick was Anderson Drive. It was a neighborhood, recalls resident Bob Summers, that had a number of close calls. It had been raining that night, Summers says. The rain ended, and he looked out a west window and saw "green fireworks" produced by snapping power lines. He left the window just before the wind blew it in. Other than broken windows the only damage to his house was a few shingles blown off. He replaced them with shingles from a roof that had been blown into his yard. Windows were also gone from the west side of his car. He found concrete blocks in the back seat. The vehicle had apparently lifted briefly because it was resting on a sheet of plywood.

After the tornado passed, Summers went out to check on his neighbors. Arriving at one home, he picked up the children, who were still in bed, and shook them to remove the glass that covered their bodies. A two-by-four had blown through the wall of another bedroom in the same home. The board rested between the pillow and the mattress. In a nearby house a babysitter had just taken an infant from its crib for a feeding. Her timing was extremely fortunate, because minutes later the tornado struck and a huge beam came down and crushed the unoccupied crib.[2]

Destruction on Anderson Drive, Brunswick. (Diane Siman)

The James Graves home, Myrtle Lane, Brunswick. (James Graves)

Two homes away, Diana (Buzek) Siman, then four years old, was in bed. "I remember hearing lots of noise," she says. Her father, Richard Buzek, heard it too, and he went to the front door "to see why a train was coming" when there was no railroad close by. As he opened the door the wind blew it off and sent him into a wall. He was "bumped and bruised" but not seriously hurt. All the windows were gone from their home, as was much of the roof. The home next door, Diana recalls, was "blown up, literally." Other houses were seriously damaged. Diana's mother, Jeanette, realized her largely intact home would likely become a gathering place for homeless neighbors. She came into Diana's room, removed the quilt from her bed, and shook off the broken glass. Later Mrs. Buzek tucked neighbor children in with her own. "Put on the tea kettle," she told her shaken husband. "We're going to need a lot of hot water."

The next day, Bob Summers notes, a number of "gawkers" descended on the neighborhood. With Jeanette he watched as one of them entered the Buzek home and left with a toaster. "Serves them right," she said. "The thing never worked."[3]

"I used to fall out of bed a lot when I was sleeping," recalls Jimmy Graves, who lived with his parents, James L. and Avonelle Graves, on Myrtle Lane in Brunswick. As a result his family bought a set of bed rails. Those rails saved him from injury and perhaps death when the tornado invaded their neighborhood, destroying his family's home and three others.

The Graveses' daughter, Linda, had been confirmed that Palm Sunday by the Methodist Church. After the service several relatives visited. Tired from the day's activities, the family went to bed early. A violent storm awakened Avonelle. She got up to open a window, fearful that it would break if she did not. As she got to it the force of the wind blew out the glass and knocked her to the floor. The glass severely cut her scalp and leg. James, still in bed and surrounded by plaster board, also suffered from cuts to the scalp. Four children were at home. None was badly hurt, but chunks of plaster hit the crib where Jeffrey, fourteen months old, was sleeping. They missed him by inches. The wall of Jimmy's bedroom came down on his bed, but the foot board and bed rails kept it from crushing him. He had about two feet of clear space to crawl out at the head of the bed. Little was left of the house. The tornado had lifted it and brought it back down off its foundation. Grass and dead birds littered the basement. The family rented a house while theirs was rebuilt. Like so many others, the Graves home attracted looters. One was scared off while attempting to wrest away the bathroom sink.[4]

Pickaway, Fairfield, and Perry Counties

The last of Ohio's major Palm Sunday storms actually struck at about

12:30 Monday morning, cutting a twenty-eight-mile damage path from west of Ashville to Somerset. In Pickaway County the damage was particularly heavy in the area near the Scioto River along State Routes 316 and 104. Nobody was killed in Pickaway County, but eleven residents of the area ended up in hospitals. Among them were seven members of one family, who were blown out into the storm when the tornado destroyed their mobile home. Both parents and one child suffered broken bones. The thirty-three-year old father was the most seriously injured. In addition to a broken arm, he had back, chest, and head injuries, plus "an enormous amount of cuts." Officials speculated that he had gone through the picture window of the home.[5]

Palm Sunday had been a day of anticipation for Rosella Hardbarger of Ashville Pike in Harrison Township. The next day Rosella, her husband, Kenneth, and their two sons, Kenneth, Jr. and George, were to leave on a vacation to Florida. As they banked their coal stove for the night, television reports said a tornado was going to hit north of Columbus. Then the weather became very hot and quiet. Soon after, "It sounded like a plane was coming." There was no time to take cover. In an instant their picture window was gone, as were the north and south walls of the house. The twister blew Rosella, who had been in the kitchen, several feet outside. The Hardbargers dashed for their car and headed south, watching utility poles fall behind them. Eventually they circled around and drove to a Columbus hospital. Only Kenneth, Jr., whose knee cap had been struck with a large piece of glass, was admitted.

Their home had to be rebuilt, and all three of their cars required repair. Most of the furniture survived. However, Rosella says, "Our stuff was scattered all over the place. It was just one big mess."[6]

Jeanne (Miller) Gray recalls waking up Monday morning, looking out the west window of her parents' home, and seeing an apple tree that had been pulled up by the roots and a peach tree split by the wind. Several bricks had also blown off their chimney. The family had slept through the storm, and, "We were just dumbfounded by that [damage]," she says. The Millers lived in Ashville. They had missed the full force of the tornado, which went north of the village. "I thought we were very lucky," she notes. A ride with her father confirmed that view. Along State Route 752 she saw numerous damaged homes. At Teays Valley High School, where she was a student, the gymnasium roof was gone and rain had ruined the floor. The school had been open three years. Despite the damage classes resumed on Wednesday.[7]

State Route 674 runs along the boundary of Pickaway and Fairfield Counties and is known locally as County Line Road. Bridget Bowen and her family lived on the east, or Fairfield County, side of the road. Across the road and to the north, in Pickaway County, were the homes of her grandparents, Norman and Ruth Pontius, and her aunt and uncle,

Ronnie and Sherrill Glick. Bridget's family slept through the storm. However, at about 4:00 a.m. Monday, Bridget's mother, Patsy Haines, heard Rick, Mr. and Mrs. Pontius's dog, barking. "My mom knew something was wrong," Bridget recalls, "by the way Rick was carrying on." She got the family up and went to see what the problem was.

"What a mess!" Bridget says. The back was of her grandparents' barn and a portion of the side wall were gone. Dead chickens dotted the barnyard. Downed electric poles took out sections of fence as they fell. From the Pontius farm the tornado had continued north to the Glick farm, which Bridget's aunt and uncle rented. Lightning had destroyed one of the two barns a few years earlier. The tornado leveled the other one. It also tore a wrap-around porch from the front and side of the house and "plucked the huge fir trees out of the ground as it went out the driveway."[8]

Continuing into Fairfield County, the tornado damaged more homes and barns. Although the twister did not result in any deaths, lightning from the storms was responsible for a fatal house fire in neighboring Hocking County. The owner, a forty-nine-year old man who lived alone, died in the blaze. In Dumontville the tornado lifted a garage and beauty shop into the air, "leaving little evidence of ever existing," according to the *Lancaster Eagle-Gazette*. At a nearby mobile home dealership on U. S. Route 33, the winds destroyed six trailers and damaged twenty-one others, causing some $40,000 in damage. The owner announced plans for a "giant storm sale." Although the tornado missed the city of Lancaster, high winds resulted in downed trees and broken windows. A truck driver received minor injuries when the wind tipped over his rig on State Route 37 north of the city.[9]

The tornado lifted near the Perry County community of Somerset. Before it did it destroyed two mobile homes and a house that was under construction. Only one of the mobile homes was occupied, and all three residents, a man, his wife, and their seven-month old son, escaped serious injury. The infant was found by his father under a mattress.[10]

Preble, Greene, and Harrison Counties

At least three other severe storms brought damaging winds to Ohio the night of the Palm Sunday outbreak. Although they may not have been tornadoes, they wreaked a fair share of havoc. One struck Preble County at about 11:30 p.m. The storm blew a 45-by-70 section of roof from the Producer's Livestock Building, located south of the county fairgrounds. "The roof was literally lifted off and set down in tepee form in an adjoining field," the *Eaton Register-Herald* reported. The wind damaged a chimney and a roof west of the Producer's Building and tore a door off a barn to the east. New Paris experienced hail "as big as a small fist," while golf ball-size hailstones fell in Lewisburg.[11]

Xenia's F5 killer tornado was nine years in the future, but a "baby tornado or twister," in the words of the *Xenia Gazette*, did an estimated $20,000 worth of damage when it struck Greene County at about midnight. Cedarville received the bulk of the damage. Residents, reported the *Gazette*, "said the approaching winds sounded like a freight train or jet airplane and lasted but a few minutes." The wind tore the roof off a house and removed porches from two others. It also blew the window out at the post office.[12]

The easternmost and last of the Palm Sunday storms struck Harrison County at about 1:30 a.m. Monday. It demolished a mobile home at Freeport, rolling it over three times and sending its owner to the hospital for cuts and bruises. In Cadiz the storm ripped the roof from a tire shop, damaged a few homes, and blew down several trees. A statue of Lady Justice sitting atop the Harrison County Courthouse was leaning about three feet. Across the street a chimney on the county jail blew off, crashing into the sheriff's car parked below.[13]

Legacy of Lifesaving

For the United States Weather Bureau, forerunner to the National Weather Service, the Palm Sunday tornadoes and their high death toll led to intense introspection. Technology, officials realized, had reached the point that it was possible to prevent many tornado deaths, even with an outbreak as extensive as this one had been. That led to a painfully obvious question: Why were 258 people dead?

Less than twenty-four hours after the storms struck, Weather Bureau officials were-- with some justification-- exonerating themselves. The Kansas City office, they pointed out, had issued forecasts for thirty-five of the thirty-seven reported Palm Sunday tornadoes. These alerts were of little use, however, if they did not reach the people in the paths of the storms. The Weather Bureau sent out a five-man survey team to determine what had been done right and wrong and how lives could be saved in the future.[14]

The team concluded that the Weather Bureau forecasts had been "very good to excellent," although they modified one earlier claim; thirty-three of the thirty-seven tornadoes had fallen within forecast areas. The team further concluded that, "The death toll would have been much higher had it not been for the excellent cooperation of the radio and TV stations in broadcasting the forecasts and warnings throughout the affected areas."

There were problems, however. While many people had heard the earlier forecasts they "did not hear the subsequent warnings" issued as the storms actually approached. One reason was that many people, taking advantage of the balmy weather, were away from radios and television sets. Another problem was that broadcast stations were minimally staffed on Sundays. Smaller stations had only one person on duty, and that individual was often unable to make frequent trips to the teletype machine to keep up with weather alerts. In the American Southwest, the report continued, the high number of tornadoes had led officials to use Civil Defense sirens "as a positive alerting device for tornado warnings." Amazingly, "None of the areas visited by the survey team had such an arrangement."[15]

Press reports at the time told readers, "The most hopeful development in tornado spotting concerns radar systems that may be able to identify tornadoes." One, the public learned, was Doppler radar "that can measure the rate of motion within a storm." Well known and widely used today, Doppler radar was sadly underutilized in 1965. "There are still important gaps in our radar network east of the Rocky Mountains," the survey team reported. In addition many of the radar systems in use "are rapidly becoming obsolete. Some," the report continued, "are in a state of disrepair, replacement parts are no longer available and it has become necessary to begin shutting down some and cannibalizing them for parts to keep more essential ones in operation." Plans were being made to replace these obsolete systems. The team suggested that those plans be carried out "with all practicable speed."[16]

Many of the weather safety measures we take for granted today grew out of the survey team's report. Among them are the NOAA twenty-four-hour weather radio system and the SKYWARN spotter program. In 1966 the Weather Bureau changed the term "tornado forecast" to "tornado watch." The "watch" and "warning" system had already been used for a decade in hurricane predictions. These improvements, along with increased public education, advances in technology, and the advent of the cable television Weather Channel, which has made us all more weather savvy, have saved countless lives. No more dramatic proof can be seen than video clips of Moore and other areas of suburban Oklahoma City following the 1999 F5 tornado. That storm caused more than twice as much property damage as any tornado ever. Yet, thanks to advance warnings, the death toll from this incredibly violent storm, which would have likely killed hundreds forty years earlier, was thirty-eight.[17]

Tornadoes can happen here, and they can be deadly. The people whose stories appear above are painfully aware of that. Fortunately, the technology to save lives is in place. But it will be only as successful as people's willingness to stay aware and heed its warnings. If this book convinces you of that fact and leads you to pay more attention to the weather and take watches and warnings seriously, it has served a valuable purpose.

Notes

Chapter 1

1. Tetsuya Fujita, Dorothy L. Bradbury, and C. F. Van Thullner, "Palm Sunday Tornadoes of April 11, 1965," *Monthly Weather Review* (January 1970), p. 29; Thomas P. Grazulus, *Significant Tornadoes, 1880-1989, Volume II: A Chronology of Events* (Environmental Films, St. Johnsbury, VT, 1990), p. 456; *New York Times*, April 13, 1965.
2. Grazulus, *Significant Tornadoes*, pp. 456-457; *Chicago Tribune*, April 12, 1965; *New York Times*, April 12-13, 1965.
3. Grazulus, *Significant Tornadoes*, p. 456; *Chicago Tribune*, April 12, 1965.
4. Grazulus, *Significant Tornadoes*, p. 460; *New York Times*, April 13, 1965.
5. *Kokomo Morning Times, Tornado 1965: Special Edition*; Grazulus, *Significant Tornadoes*, p. 460.
6. *Elkhart Truth, Tornado: A Report on the Palm Sunday Disaster and its Aftermath*, pp. 17-18; *New York Times*, April 13, 1965.
7. *Elkhart Truth, Tornado*, p. 18; Debbie Watters, unpublished reminiscences.
8. Grazulus, *Significant Tornadoes*, pp. 459, 460, 464, 465; *Hillsdale Daily News*, April 12, 1965.
9. Grazulus, *Significant Tornadoes*, p. 459; *Hillsdale Daily News*, April 12, 1965.
10. Ibid., April 13, 1965.
11. Int. with Fred Sprang, October 20, 2002; int. with Sandra Compton, September 29, 2002.
12. Int. with Greg Ross, September 25, 2002; int. with Darrel Scharp, September 29, 2002.
13. Int. with Kenneth Coe, October 29, 2002.
14. *Hillsdale Daily News*, April 14, 1965.
15. Int. with Daniel Watkins, September 25, 2002.
16. Int. with John M. Fullerton, September 29, 2002.
17. Int. with Philip B. and Pat Fleming, September 26, 2002.
18. *Adrian Telegram*, April 12, 14, 1965.
19. Ibid., April 12, 1965; int. with Barbara Reyes, September 30, 2002.
20. *Adrian Telegram*, April 14, 1965; int. with Viloet Waltz, September 30, 2002.
21. *Adrian Telegram*, April 12, 14, 1965.
22. *Congressional Record*, June 3, 1965.

Chapter 2

1. *Bluffton News-Banner*, April 12, 1965.
2. Int. with Waneta Cooper, September 26, 2002.
3. Int. with Alice Ann Norris Van Wagner, October 29, 2002.
4. *Decatur Democrat*, April 19, 1965; int. with Melissa Fey, October 31, 2002.
5. *Berne Witness*, April 14, 1965.
6. Int. with John F. and Judy Habegger, September 14, 2002.
7. *Berne Witness*, April 14, 1965.
8. Sue (Riesen) Koehler to RP, October 28, 2002; Kathy Riesen vance to RP, November 13, 2002.
9. *Berne Witness*, April 14, 1965.
10. Int. with Ken Selking, October 31, 2002.

11. Int. with Joe Smekens, October 28, 2002.
12. Int. with Larry Lautzenheiser, October 20, 2002.
13. *Celina Daily Standard*, April 12, 1965; int. with Linda Tricker, September 25, 2002.
14. *Rockford Press*, April 15, 1965; int. with John E. Vining, September 14, 2002.
15. Int. with Duane Hamrick, September 15, 2002.
16. *VanWert Times-Bulletin*, April 12, 1965.
17. Int. with Irene A. Kill, November 29, 2002.
18. Int. with Cheryl Freewalt, July 13, 2002; int. with Carol Place, September 22, 2002.

Chapter 3

1. Int. with Keaton Vandemark, July 8, 2002.
2. Int. with Tom and Jane Miller, July 11, 2002; int. with Keaton Vandemark, July 8, 2002; *Lima News*, April 14, 1965.
3. Int. with Tom and Jane Miller, July 11, 2002; int. with Keaton Vandemark, July 8, 2002.
4. *Lima News*, April 13, 1965; Grazulus, *Significant Tornadoes*, p. 465.
5. Int. with Mike Grove, October 21, 2002; int. with Mike Roeder, September 15, 2002.
6. Int. with Larry Hurley, July 11, 2002.
7. *Lima News*, April 12, 14, 1965.
8. Margaret Rusmisel, "Could That Pile of Rubble Be the House?" *Farmland News*, April 11, 1989, p. 3; int. with David and Margaret Rusmisel, December 11, 2002.
9. *Lima News*, April 15, 1965.
10. Int. with Rex Ferrall, September 14, 2002.
11. Int. with Doyt and Wilda Hanthorn, September 23, 2002.
12. Int. with Fred Arnold, September 14, 2002.
13. Int. with Mike Allgire, July 11, 2002.
14. Int. with Joyce Beery, October 3, 2002.
15. Int. with Charles and Janice Amstutz, September 14, 2002.
16. Int. with Carol Bell, December 8, 2002; int. with Ralph Quellhorst, December 8, 2002.
17. *Findlay Republican-Courier*, April 12, 1965; int. with Barbara L. Smith, July 13, 2002.
18. Int. with Robert K. Flick, October 28, 2002.
19. *Tiffin Advertiser-Tribune*, April 13, 1965.
20. *Republic Reporter*, April 15, 1965; int. with Dan Leibengood, July 22, 2002.
21. *Republic Reporter*, April 15, 1965; int. with Larry T. Egbert and Donna K. Fox, July 22, 2002.
22. Int. with Herval Thalman, July 22, 2002.
23. Int. with Mildred Biller, July 22, 2002.

Chapter 4

1. *Toledo Blade*, April 12, 1965.
2. Int. with Ken and Virginia Rutkowski, July 13, 2002.
3. Int. with William Bettinger, July 21, 2002.
4. *Toledo Blade*, April 14, 1965; int. with Jerry Extine and Joyce Ruch, July 21, 2002.
5. Int. with Myron Jones, September 25, 2002.
6. *Toledo Blade*, April 12, 14, 16, 1965; int. with Isador Perlmutter, November 9, 2002.
7. Int. with Barbara Jones, September 25, 2002; *Toledo Blade*, April 12, 1965.
8. Int. with Gene, Betty, and Mike Cerveny, June 14, 2002.

9. Int. with Paul D. Smith, June 14, 2002; John Smith, "My Story," *Dare to Care*, a publication of HCR Manor Care, March 2001.
10. *Toledo Blade*, April 12, 1965.
11. Int. with Nancy Schill and Don Loucks, June 14, 2002.
12. Int. with Sam Foremen, October 6, 2002.
13. *Monroe Evening News*, April 12, 13, 1965.
14. Ibid., April 12, 1965; int. with Fred Abair, October 8, 2002.
15. Int. with Dick Rombkowski, September 24, 2002; int. with Karen Skelton, Kim Johnson, and Cindy Roach, July 21, 2002.

Chapter 5

1. Grazulus, *Significant Tornadoes*, p. 465; *Sidney News*, April 12, 17, 1965.
2. Ibid., April 13, 14, 17, 1965.
3. Int. with Melba and Roger Bender, Joyce Porter, and Bonnie Josefovsky, August 17, 2002.
4. Int. with Tim Ernst, October 29, 2002.
5. Int. with Don and Phyl Puthoff, and Jeannie Snarr, August 17, 2002.
6. Int. with Tom R. Niekamp, December 26, 2002.
7. Int. with Jon Blakley, June 17, 2002; *Sidney News*, April 13, 1965.
8. Int. with Robert Riggs, June 17, 2002; int. with James and Betty Riggs, July 13, 2002; *Sidney News*, April 15, 2002.
9. Int. with Roger Lantz, October 29, 2002.
10. Int. with Phyllis Lackey, July 11, 2002.
11. *Delaware Gazette*, April 12, 1965; *Columbus Dispatch*, April 13, 1965.
12. Int. with Don and Pat Spriggs, September 28, 2002.
13. Int. with Don R. and Eloise Stutler, July 10, 2002.
14. Int. with David and Vicki James, July 10, 2002.
15. Int. with George R. Thomas, July 10, 2002.
16. Int. with R. Bruce McKibben, August 17, 2002; *Columbus Dispatch*, April 13, 1965.
17. Int. with Don, Dorothy, and Dennis Kaelber and Debbie Caudill, July 10, 2002.
18. Int. with John and Maxine Moore, July 10, 2002.
20. Int. with Gladys Geesey, July 10, 2002.
19. Int. with Sue Snavley, July 10, 2002.
21. [Mt. Gilead] *Morrow County Sentinel*, April 15, 1965; *Marion Star*, April 12, 1965; [Cardington] *Morrow County Independent*, April 15, 1965.
22. Int. with Tom and Doris Crump, August 16, 2002; int. with Noreena Taylor, October 23, 2002.
23. Int. with Miriam Newell, July 10, 2002.

Chapter 6

1. Grazulus, *Significant Tornadoes*, p. 466.
2. Int. with Charles and Linda Knapp and Sherry (Knapp) Norton, October 12, 2002.
3. Int. with Dave and Gerry Nash and Cathy (Nash) Bowman, June 24, 2002.
4. Int. with Anne Broud, June 23, 2002.
5. *Elyria Chronicle-Telegram*, April 12, 1965; *Wellington Enterprise*, April 15, 1965.
6. *Lorain Journal*, April 13, 1965.

7. Ibid.
8. *Elyria Chronicle-Telegram*, April 12, 1965; *Wellington Enterprise*, April 15, 1965.
9. Int. with Rev. Elmer and Ruth Novak, December 21, 2002.
10. Int. with Robert Diedrick, October 13, 2002; int. with Paul O. Pickworth, October 21, 2002.
11. Int. with Caroline Harris and Mrs. Elmer Harris, June 24, 2002.
12. Int. with Charles Jackson, October 13, 2002.
13. Int. with Perry Brandt, June 24, 2002.
14. Int. with Jean McConnell, June 23, 2002.
15. Int. with Jim Sheffield, June 23, 2002.
16. Int. with Robert Diedrick, October 13, 2002.
17. Int. with Phyllis Langdon, October 12, 2002.
18. Int. with Donna Sears, October 12, 2002.
19. Int. with Wendell F. Cotton, October 21, 2002; int. with Tyler Cotton, November 6, 2002; int. with Brad Cotton, October 28, 2002; int. with Ryan Cotton, July 14, 2002; int. with Corinne Precourt, October 28, 2002.
20. Int. with Norma Roberts, July 13, 2002.
21. Int. with Dorothy George, June 24, 2002.
22. *Oberlin News-Tribune*, April 15, 1965; *Lorain Journal*, April 15, 16, 19, 1965; *Elyria Chronicle-Telegram*, April 15, 1965.
23. *Oberlin News-Tribune*, April 15, 1965; *Elyria Chronicle-Telegram*, April 19, 1965; int. with Rev. Elmer Novak, December 21, 2002.
24. *Elyria Chronicle-Telegram*, April 13, 14, 1965; *Lorain Journal*, April 15, 1965; *Wellington Enterprise*, April 15, 1965.
25. Int. with Ed Burke, June 23, 2002.
26. Int. with Kathy, Rosemary, and Martha Zalka, June 23, 2002.
27. Int. with Marla Koviak, June 24, 2002.
28. Int. with Ellie Marsh, July 13, 2002.
29. Int. with John Poulton, October 12, 2002.
30. Int. with Jim Seabold, October 21, 2002; int. with Judi and Emily Buga, October 12, 2002.
31. *Elyria Chronicle-Telegram*, April 13-14, 1965; int. with Mrs. Elmer Harris, June 24, 2002.
32. Int. with Robert Meyer, June 24, 2002.
33. Int. with Ruth Grobske, June 28, 2002.
34. Int. with Bernadine Kubuski, Nancy Caithaml, Margie Toombs, and Tom Kubuski, October 13, 2002.
35. Int. with Jeff Wagamon, June 23, 2002.
36. Int. with Bill Heidinger, December 27, 2002; int. with Craig Heidinger, June 23, 2002.
37. *Cleveland Plain Dealer,* April 12-13, 1965.
38. Int. with Dorothy Klotzsche, December 26, 2002.
39. Int. with Alvin Van Bumble, December 26, 2002.
40. Int. with Rusty Taphous, June 23, 2002.
41. Int. with Pat Hoke, July 14, 2002.

Chapter 7

1. Grazulus, *Significant Tornadoes*, p. 466; *Elyria Chronicle-Telegram*, April 14, 1965.

2. Int. with Bob Summers, October 13, 2002.
3. Int. with Diana Siman, October 13, 2002; int. with Bob Summers, October 13, 2002.
4. Int. with James L. and Avonelle Graves, October 12, 2002.
5. [Ashville] *Pickaway County News*, April 15, 1965.
6. Int. with Rosella Hardbarger, October 28, 2002.
7. Int. with Jeanne Gray, October 28, 2002.
8. Bridget Bowen, letter to R. P., September 14, 2002.
9. *Lancaster Eagle-Gazette*, April 12, 1965.
10. *Columbus Dispatch*, April 13, 1965.
11. *Eaton Register-Herald*, April 14, 1965.
12. *Xenia Gazette*, April 12, 1965.
13. *Cadiz Republican*, April 15, 1965.
14. *New York Times*, April 12-13, 1965.
15. United States Weather Bureau, *Weather Bureau Survey Team Report of Palm Sunday Tornadoes of 1965* (Washington, D. C., 1965), pp. 1, 3, 4.
16. *New York Times*, April 13, 1965; U. S. Weather Bureau, *Survey Team Report*, p. 10.
17. Thomas P. Grazulus, *The Tornado: Nature's Ultimate Wimdstorm* (Norman, OK, 2001), pp. 91, 206.

Bibliography

Interviews

Abair, Fred, October 8, 2002
Allgire, Mike, July 11, 2002
Amstutz, Charles and Janice, September 14, 2002
Arnold, Fred, September 14, 2002
Bell, Carol, December 8, 2002
Bender, Melba and Roger, August 17, 2002
Beery, Joyce, October 3, 2002
Bettinger, William, July 21, 2002
Biller, Mildred, July 22, 2002
Blakley, Jon, June 17, 2002
Bowman, Cathy, June 24, 2002
Brandt, Perry, June 24, 2002
Broud, Anne, June 23, 2002
Buga, Judi and Emily, October 12, 2002
Burke, Ed, June 23, 2002
Caithaml, Nancy, October 13, 2002
Caudill, Debbie, July 10, 2002
Cerveny, Gene, Betty, and Mike, June 14, 2002
Coe, Kenneth, October 29, 2002
Compton, Sandra, September 29, 2002
Cooper, Waneta, September 26, 2002
Cotton, Brad, October 28, 2002
Cotton, Ryan, July 14, 2002
Cotton, Tyler, November 6, 2002
Cotton, Wendell F., October 21, 2002
Crump, Tom and Doris, August 16, 2002
Diedrick, Robert, October 13, 2002
Egbert, Larry T., July 22, 2002
Ernst, Tim, October 29, 2002
Extine, Jerry, July 21, 2002
Ferrall, Rex, September 14, 2002
Fey, Melissa, October 31, 2002
Fleming, Philip B. and Pat, September 26, 2002
Flick, Robert K., October 28, 2002
Foreman, Sam, October 6, 2002
Fox, Donna K., July 22, 2002
Freewalt, Cheryl, July 13, 2002
Fullerton, John M., September 29, 2002
Geesey, Gladys, July 10, 2002
George, Dorothy, June 24, 2002
Graves, James L. and Avonelle, October 12, 2002
Gray, Jeanne, October 28, 2002
Grobske, Ruth, June 28, 2002
Grove, Mike, October 21, 2002

Habegger, John F. and Judy, September 14, 2002
Hanthorn, Doyt and Wilda, September 23, 2002
Hamrick, Duane, September 15, 2002
Hardbarger, Rosella, October 28, 2002
Harris, Mrs. Elmer and Caroline, June 24, 2002
Heidinger, Bill, December 27, 2002
Heidinger, Craig, June 23, 2002
Hoke, Pat, July 14, 2002
Hurley, Larry, July 11, 2002
Jackson, Charles, October 13, 2002
James, David and Vicki, July 10, 2002
Johnson, Kim, July 21, 2002
Jones, Myron and Barbara, September 25, 2002
Josefovsky, Bonnie, August 17, 2002
Kaelber, Don, Dorothy, and Dennis, July 10, 2002
Kill, Irene A., November 29, 2002
Klotzsche, Dorothy, December 26, 2002
Knapp, Charles and Linda, October 12, 2002
Koviak, Marla, June 24, 2002
Kubuski, Bernadine and Tom, October 13, 2002
Lackey, Phyllis, July 11, 2002
Langdon, Phyllis, October 12, 2002
Lantz, Roger, October 29, 2002
Lautzenheiser, October 20, 2002
Leibengood, Dan, July 22, 2002
Loucks, Don, June 14, 2002
Marsh, Ellie, July 13, 2002
McConnell, Jean, June 23, 2002
McKibben, R. Bruce, August 17, 2002
Meyer, Robert, June 24, 2002
Miller, Tom and Jane, July 11, 2002
Moore, John and Maxine, July 10, 2002
Nash, Dave and Gerry, June 24, 2002
Newell, Miriam, July 10, 2002
Niekamp, Tom R., December 26, 2002
Norton, Sherry, October 12, 2002
Novak, Rev. Elmer and Ruth, December 21, 2002
Perlmutter, Isador, November 9, 2002
Pickworth, Paul O., October 21, 2002
Place, Carol, September 22, 2002
Porter, Joyce, August 17, 2002
Poulton, John, October 12, 2002
Precourt, Corinne, October 28, 2002
Puthoff, Don and Phyl, August 17, 2002
Quellhorst, Ralph, December 8, 2002
Reyes, Barbara, September 30, 2002
Riggs, James and Betty, July 13, 2002
Riggs, Robert, June 17, 2002

Roach, Cindy, July 21, 2002
Roberts, Norma, July 13, 2002
Roeder, Mike, September 15, 2002
Rombkowski, Dick, September 24, 2002
Ross, Greg, September 25, 2002
Ruch, Joyce, July 21, 2002
Rusmisel, David and Margaret, December 11, 2002
Rutkowski, Ken and Virginia, July 13, 2002
Scharp, Darrel, September 29, 2002
Schill, Nancy, June 14, 2002
Seabold, Jim, October 21, 2002
Sears, Donna, October 12, 2002
Selking, Ken, October 31, 2002
Sheffield, Jim, June 23, 2002
Siman, Diana, October 13, 2002
Skelton, Karen, July 21, 2002
Smekens, Joe, October 28, 2002
Smith, Barbara L., July 13, 2002
Smith, Paul D., June 14, 2002
Snarr, Jeannie, August 17, 2002
Snavley, Sue, July 10, 2002
Sprang, Fred, October 20, 2002
Spriggs, Don and Pat, September 28, 2002
Stutler, Don R. and Eloise, July 10, 2002
Summers, Bob, October 13, 2002
Taphous, Rusty, June 23, 2002
Taylor, Noreena, October 23, 2002
Thalman, Herval, July 22, 2002
Thomas, George R., July 10, 2002
Toombs, Margie, October 13, 2002
Tricker, Linda, September 25, 2002
Van Bumble, Alvin, December 26, 2002
Van Wagner, Alice Ann Norris, October 29, 2002
Vandemark Keaton, July 8, 2002
Vining, John E., September 14, 2002
Wagamon, Jeff, June 23, 2002
Watkins, Daniel, September 25, 2002
Zalka, Kathy, Rosemary, and Martha, June 23, 2002

Letters and other unpublished sources

Bowen, Bridget, to RP, September 14, 2002.
Koehler, Sue, to RP, October 28, 2002.
Vance, Kathy to RP, November 13, 2002.
Watters, Debbie, unpublished reminiscences.

Newspapers

Adrian [Michigan] Telegram
[Ashville] *Pickaway County News*
Berne [Indiana] Witness
Bluffton [Indiana] News-Banner
Cadiz Republican
[Cardington] *Morrow County Independent*
Celina Standard
Chicago Tribune
Cleveland Plain Dealer
Columbus Dispatch
Decatur [Indiana] Democrat
Delaware Gazette
Eaton Register-Herald
Elkhart [Indiana] Truth
Elyria Chronicle-Telegram
Findlay Republican-Courier
Hillsdale [Michigan] News
Kokomo [Indiana] Times
Lancaster Eagle-Gazette
Lima News
Lorain Journal
Marion Star
Monroe [Michigan] Evening News
[Mt. Gilead] *Morrow County Sentinel*
New York Times
Oberlin News-Tribune
Republic Reporter
Rockford Press
Sidney News
Tiffin Advertiser-Tribune
Toledo Blade
Van Wert Times-Bulletin
Xenia Gazette
Wellington Enterprise

Books and Articles

Fujita, Tetsuya, Dorothy L. Bradbury, and C. F. Van Thullner, "Palm Sunday Tornadoes of April 11, 1965," *Monthly Weather Review* (January 1970).
Grazulus, Thomas P., *Significant Tornadoes, 1880-1989, Volume II: A Chronology of Events* (St. Johnsbuty, VT, 1990).
_____, *The Tornado: Nature's Ultimate Windstorm* (Norman, OK, 2001).
Rusmisel, Margaret, "Could That Pile of Rubble Be the House?" *Farmland News*, April 11, 1989.
United States Weather Bureau, *Weather Bureau Survey Team Report of Palm Sunday Tornadoes of 1965* (Washington, D.C., 1965).

Index

Abair, Bernadine 56
Abair, Fred 56
Adams County, IN 17-23
Allen County, OH 27-38
Allen Memorial Hospital 89
Allgire, Mike 35
Allgire, Susan 35
Allgire, Vera 35
Allgire, Virgil 35
Alto, IN 2-3, 6-7
Alvada, OH 40
American Red Cross 9, 35, 56, 68, 73
Amstutz, Charles W. 36-37
Amstutz, Janice 36
Amstutz, Wilbur 36
Arnold, Ann 34
Arnold, Fred 34-35
Arnold, Mark 34
Arnold, Merrill 34
Arnold, Pat 34
Arnold, Velma 34
Ashville, OH 105

Baldwin-Wallace College 100
Baltimore & Ohio Railroad 59
Bankers, MI 10-11
Barlow, Gene 81
Baw Beese Lake 11, 12, 13
Beale, Ruth 57-58
Bear Lake 8, 10
Beaverdam, OH 33-35
Beck, Walt 34-35
Beery, Joyce 35-36
Begg, Bill 35
Bell, Carol 37-38
Bell, Tom 37
Bender, Dan 59-60
Bender, Martin 59-60
Bender, Melba 59-60
Bender, Roger 59-60
Berne, IN 22
Bettinger, Harold 46-47
Bettinger, Leonard 46-47
Bettinger, Suzanne 47
Bettinger, William 47
Bettinger Farms & Greenhouse, Inc. 46-47
Biller, Jim 44-45

Biller, Mildred 44-45
Biller, Wayne 44-45
Bittner, Mayor Maurice 94
Blackford County, IN 16
Blakley, Jon 61-62
Bluffton, OH 28, 36, 38
Bonanza, TV series 25, 35, 39, 49, 77
Boone County, IN 2
Boutwell, Wanda 34
Boutwell, Willis 34
Bowen, Bridget 105-106
Bowman, Cathy 77
Bradley, Ray 85
Branch County, MI 8
Brandt, Bonnie 84
Brandt, Lois 84
Brandt, Nancy 84
Brandt, Perry 84
Broud, Anne 78
Brunswick, OH 102-104
Buga, Mrs. Frank 94
Buga, Judi 93-94
Burke, Ed 91-92
Burke, Linda 91
Burns, Sheriff Robert 59
Buzek, Jeanette 104
Buzek, Richard 104

Cairo, OH 29, 31
Caithaml, Nancy 95, 97
Cadiz, OH 107
Caton, Woody L. 3
Caudill, Debbie 72
Cedar County, IO 1
Cedarville, OH 107
Cerveny, Betty 49-50
Cerveny, Gene 49-50
Clinton County, IO 1
Clymer, Eva 35-36
Coe, Kenneth 11-12
Coldwater Lake 8
Columbia Station, OH 98-99
Compton, Sandra 8-9
Cooper, Samuel F. 16-17
Cooper, Waneta 16-17
Cotton, Brad 87-88
Cotton, Marie F. 86-88
Cotton, Ryan 87-88

Cotton, Tyler 87-88
Cotton, Wendell F. 86-88
Cowling, Garnard 78
Creekside Addition 49-52
Crump, Andrew 73-74
Crump, Doris 73-74
Crump, Keith 74
Crump, Tom 73-74
Crystal Lake, IL 1-2
Cuyahoga County, OH 99-101

Decatur, IN 22
Delaware County, OH 67-73, 75
Delphos, OH 26
Depinet, Bob 45
Dewey, Carl 84
Dewey, Catherine 84
Dewey, Richard 78, 84
Dewey, Sandra 78
Dewey, Stephen 78-79
Devil's Lake 13-14
Diedrick, Betty 85
Diedrick, Robert 80, 85
Diedrick, Robert J. 85, 86
Doppler radar 108
Dumontville, OH 106
Dunlap, IN 3-5

East Gilead, MI 8
Egbert, Catherine 41-42
Egbert, Donald 41-42
Egbert, Larry T. 41-42
Elgin High School 71
Elkhart, IN 3-5
Elkhart County, IN 3-5
Elyria Memorial Hospital 78
Ernst, Tim 60
Evard, Frank N. 90
Extine, Edward 47-48
Extine, Jerry 47-48
Extine, John 47-48

Fairfield County, OH 105-106
Ferrall, Nettie 33
Ferrall, Rex 33
Ferrall, Vicki 33
Fetters, Ken 23
Fetters, Marianna 23
Fey, Melissa 17-18

Fleming, Pat 12-13
Fleming, Dr. Philip B. 12-13
Flick, Mark A. 39-40
Flick, Mary E. 39-40
Flick, Mary Kathleen 39-40
Flick, Robert K. 39-40
Flick, Thomas L. 39-40
Foreman, Sandy 53
Foreman, Sam 53, 56
Forsythe, Charles 3-5
Forsythe, Mike 3-5
Forsythe, Shirley 3-5
Forsythe, Steve 3-5
Fox, Donna K. 44
Freeport, OH 107
Freewalt, Cheryl 25-26
Fort Loramie, OH 59, 60
Fullerton, John M. 12

Geesey, Gladys 73, 75
George, Dorothy 89
Gibbons, Bruce 90-91
Gibbons, Elsie 90-91
Gibbs, Beverly 14
Gibbs, Fred 14
Gibbs, Garaldine 14
Gibbs, Ruth 14
Glick, Ronnie 106
Glick, Sherrill 106
Goddard, Dick 85
Gomer, OH 28, 31
Gotts, Duane 92
Goubeaux, Leo 60
Goubeaux, Sis 60
Grady Hospital 70, 72
Grafton, OH 94-97
Grand Rapids, MI 7
Grandlienard, Dale 17-18
Grandlienard, Izzy 17-18
Grandlienard, Judy 17-18
Grandlienard, Steve 17-18
Grant County, IN 2-3
Graves, Avonelle 104
Graves, James L. 103, 104
Graves, Jeffrey 104
Graves, Jimmy 104
Graves, Linda 104
Gray, Jeanne 105
Grazulus, Thomas 76
Green County, WI 1
Greene County, OH 107
Greentown, IN 3

Gregg, Evelyn M. 15
Grobske, D. John 94-95
Grobske, Ruth 94-95
Grove, Mike 28-29
Grubbs, Beverly 13-14
Grubbs, Carolyn 13-14
Grubbs, Harold 13-14

Habegger, Dawn 18-19
Habegger, John F. 18-19
Habegger, Judy 18-19
Haines, Patsy 106
Hamilton County, IN 2
Hamrick, Barbara 24
Hamrick, Duane 24
Hancock County, OH 38-40
Hanthorn, Doyt 33-34
Hanthorn, Mary 33-34
Hanthorn, Sandra 33-34
Hanthorn, Susan 33-34
Hanthorn, Wilda 33-34
Hardbarger, George 105
Hardbarger, Kenneth 105
Hardbarger, Kenneth, Jr. 105
Hardbarger, Rosella 105
Harrington, Charles G. 56
Harris, Caroline M. 81
Harris, David 81
Harris, Deborah 16-17
Harris, Mrs. Elmer 81, 94
Harris, Helen 81
Harris, Susan 16-17
Harris, Warren 81
Harrison County, OH 107
Heidinger, Bill 98
Heidinger, Craig 98-99
Heimerdinger, Clarence 15
Hillsdale County, MI 8-13
Hinckley, OH 102
Hocking County, OH 106
Hoke, Pat 100
Howard County, IN 2-3
Hurley, Larry 29
Hurley, Richard 29
Hurley, Ruth 29

Illinois 1-2
Indiana 2-7, 16-23
Iowa 1

Jackson, Barbara 81
Jackson, Charles 81, 82

Jackson County, IO 1
James, Bob 71
James, David 68-69
James, Glenn 71
James, Lori Ann 68-69
James, Mark 68-69
James, Vicki 68-69
Jefferson County, WI 1
Jenera, OH 28
Johnson, Kim 57-58
Joiner, George 45
Joiner, Rosella 45
Jones, Barbara 49
Jones, Ed 27
Jones, Florence 27
Jones, Myron 48
Josefovsky, Bonnie 59-60

Kaelber, Dennis 72
Kaelber, Diane 72
Kaelber, Don 72
Kaelber, Dorothy 72
Katz, Samuel B. 90
Kent County, MI 7
Kepler, Lou 78
Keystone, IN 16-17
Keystone Friends Church 16
Kill, Daniel 25
Kill, Irene A. 25
Kill, Linus 25
Kill, Mary Lou 25
Klier, Louis 79
Klockowski, Debbie 57
Klotzsche, Dorothy 99
Klotzche, Richard 99
Knapp, Bonny 76
Knapp, Charles 76
Knapp, David 76
Knapp, Linda 76
Knierieman, Lorin 41
Kokomo, IN 2-3
Koviak, Marla 92-93
Kubuski, Bernadine 95, 97
Kubuski, Ed 95, 97
Kubuski, Tom 95, 97

Lackey, Don 67
Lackey, Phyllis 67
Laderach, Irene 57-58
Lagrange, OH 90-94
La Grange County, IN 3-5
Lancaster, OH 106
Langdon, Howard 85
Langdon, Kenneth 85

Langdon, Phyllis 85
Lantz, Gary 63, 67
Lantz, Roger 63, 67
Lashaway, Irma 56
Lautzenheiser, Larry 22-23
Lautsenheiser, Linda 22-23
Lebanon, IN 2
Leibengood, Alan 40-41
Leibengood, Dan 40-41
Leibengood, Francis 40-41
Leibengood, Mary 40-41
Leibengood, Theresa 40-41
Lenawee County, MI 8, 13-15
Lewisburg, OH 106
Linn Grove, IN 17-19
looters 9, 27-28, 58, 62, 69, 77, 98, 104
Lorain County, OH 76-99
Lost Peninsula 56-58
Loucks, Bob 53
Loucks, Don 52-53
Lucas County, OH 46-56

Manitou Beach, MI 13-14
Manitou Beach Bible Church 13
Maplewood, OH 59
Marion, IN 3
Marsh, Douglas 93
Marsh, Ellie 93
Marsh, Gregory 93
Marsh, Marvin 93
Marshall County, IN 3
McConnell, Howard 84
McConnell, Jean 84
McConnell, Mark 84
McKibben, R. Bruce 70-72
McKibben, Marjorie 71-72
McKibben, Richard 71-72
Medina County, OH 102
Mercer County, OH 23-24, 25-26
Mercy Hospital 41
Meyer, Robert 94
Michigan 7-15, 56-58
Middleburg Heights, OH 99
Midview High School 97
Miller, Edith 27
Miller, Jane 27-28
Miller, Kenny 27
Miller, Noah 27
Miller, Oletha 27

Miller, Tom 27
Mills, Alice 84
Minster, OH 59
Moore, John 72-73
Moore, Maxine 72-73
Monroe, WI 1
Monroe County, MI 8, 56-58
Montgomery County, IN 2
Morrow County, OH 73-75
Mottinger, Mayor Vaughn 25

Nash, Dave 77, 82
Nash, Gerry 77
Nash, Kim 77
New Haven, IN 22
New Paris, OH 106
New York Central RR 48
Newell, Cecil 75
Newell, Larry 74-75
Newell, Miriam 74-75
Niekamp, Angela 61
Niekamp, Daniel 61
Niekamp, Mary 61
Niekamp, Tom. R. 61
Norris, Alfred 17
Norris, Betsy Annette 17
North Adams, MI 11
Norton, Sherry 76
Novak, Benjamin 79-80
Novak Rev. Elmer 79-80, 90
Novak, Ruth 79-80

Oberlin, OH 89
Oberlin College 81, 90
Oberlin High School 90
O'Hare Int. Airport 2
Ohio City, OH 25
Onsted, MI 14
Ottawa County, MI 7
Ottawa River 52, 56, 58

Pendleton, Martha 94
Perlmutter, Isadore 49
Perlmutter, Marion 49
Perry County, OH 106
Pickaway County, OH 104-106
Pickworth, Clayton 80-81
Pickworth, Paul O. 80-81
Pittsfield, OH 78-85, 89, 90, 94
Pittsfield Community Church 90

Place, Carol 26
Pontius, Norman 105-106
Pontius, Ruth 105-106
Porter, Joyce 59-60
Poulton, John 93
Poulton, Rodney 93
Preble County, OH 106
Precourt, Corinne 87-88
Puthoff, Don 60-61
Puthoff, Phyl 60-61

Quellhorst, Cindy 37-38
Quellhorst, Mindy 37-38
Quellhorst, Ralph 37-38
Quellhorst, Sue 37-38

Radnor, OH 67-72
Reading, MI 8
Reichenbach, Betty 35-36
Reichenbach, Richard 35-36
Reichenbach, Ulysses 35-36
Republic, OH 44
Reyes, Barbara 13-14
Rhodes, Gov. James A. 78
Riesen, Sue 19-20
Riesen, Tom 19-20
Riggs, Betty 62-63
Riggs, James 62-63
Riggs, James, Jr. 62-63
Riggs, Jeffrey, 62-63
Riggs, Jerry 62-63
Riggs, John 62-63
Riggs, Kenneth 62-63
Riggs, Rita 62-63
Riggs, Robert 62-63
Riverside Hospital 53
Roach, Cindy 57-58
Roberts, Francis 88
Roberts, Norma 88-89
Robey, Eva 79, 81
Rockaway, OH 40-44
Rockford, OH 24
Roeder, Mike 28-29
Rombkowski, Chere 57-58
Rombkowski, Dick 57-58
Ross, Greg 10-11
Ruch, Joyce 48
Rusmisel, David 32-33
Rusmisel, Laura 32-33
Rusmisel, Margaret 32-33
Rusmisel, Paul 32-33
Rusmisel, Verna 32-33
Russiaville, IN 2, 6

Rutkowski, Ken 46
Rutkowski, Virginia 46

St. Joseph County, IN 3
St. Joseph School 99, 101
St. Mary's-on-the-Lake Church 13
Salvation Army 9
Scharp, Darrel 11
Schill, Bill 52-53, 54
Schill, Nancy 52-53, 54
Seabold, Jim 93
Sears, Donna 86
Selking, Ken 22
Seneca County, OH 40-45
Sheffield, Amy 84-85
Sheffield, Henry 84-85
Sheffield, Jim 84-85
Sheffield, Tom 84-85
Shelby County, OH 59-67
Sheldon, Leona B. 39
Sheridan, IN 2
Siman, Diana 104
Skelton, Karen 57
Smekens, Joe 22
Smith, Barbara L. 39
Smith, Homer 29, 32
Smith, John 50-52
Smith, June 29
Smith, Paul 50-52
Smith, Paul D. 50-52
Smith, Sherrie 50-52
Smith, Shirley 50
Snarr, Jeanne 61
Snavley, Sue 73
Somerset, OH 105, 106
Southern Lorain County Hospital 88-89
Southwest Community Hospital 99
Speake, Leon 91, 92
Sprang, Carolyn 8
Sprang, Fred 8-9
Sprang, Sarah 8-9
Spriggs, Donald 67-68
Spriggs, Gene 67-68
Spriggs, Pat 67-68
Spriggs, Rex 67-68
Starke County, IN 3
Steiner, Betty 37
Steiner, Evan 37
Steiner, Greg 37
Steiner, JIm 35-36

Steiner, Joe 35-36
Steiner, John 35-36
Steiner, Sally 36
Stipp, Bethany 79
Strong, Hope 29
Strongsville, OH 99-101
Stutler, Don 68
Stutler, Don R. 68
Stutler, Mary 68
Summers, Bob 102
Sutter, Ed 34
Swanders, OH 59
Swank, Arthur 36-37
Swank, Edith 36-37
Swayzee, IN 3

Taphous, Harold 100
Taphous, La Verne 100
Taphous, Rusty 100
Tarr, Ray 53
Taylor, Noreena 73-74
Teays Valley High School 105
Thallman, Claudine 44
Thallman, Harval 44
Thomas, Fern 69-70
Thomas, George R. 69-70
Thomas, George W. 69-70
Thomas, Mary Ann 69-70
Tipton, MI 14
Toledo, OH 46-58
Toombs, Margie 95, 97
Trevathan, Dennis 10-11
Tricker, Linda 23
Tuscola County, MI 15

Union County, OH 67
United States Weather Bureau 107-108

Van Bumble, Alvin 99-100
Van Wagner, Alice Ann 17
Van Wert County, OH 24-26

Vance, Kathy 19-20
Vandemark, Clair 27-28, 30
Vandemark, Elsie 27-28
Vandemark, Keaton 27-28
Venedocia, OH 26
Vining, Eugene 23-24
Vining, John E. 23-24
Vining, Rosella 23-24

Wagamon, Beatrice 97-98
Wagamon, J. C. 97-98
Wagamon, Jeff 97-98
Waldo Methodist Church 72
Walnut Grove Methodist Church 24-25
Waltz, Violet 14
Ward, Prof. Addison 79, 85, 88
Ward, Peter 79, 85
Watertown, WI 1
Watkins, Daniel 12
Watters, Debbie 3-5
Webb, Gaylord 40
Weiler, Sheriff Richard 7
Wells County, IN 16-17
Wellington, OH 88, 89
Westfield, OH 72, 73-74
Wilson, Fern 73
Wilson, Horace 73
Wilson, James C. 91
Wilson Memorial Hospital 61
Wisconsin 1
Wolfe, Matthew 23
Wolfe, Phyllis 23
Wolfe, Robert 23

Xenia, OH 107

Ypsilanti, MI 11

Zalka, Joe 91
Zalka, Kathy 92
Zalka, Martha 92
Zalka, Rosemary 91-92

BUCKEYE BLIZZARD:

Ohio and the 1950 Thanksgiving Storm

When a team of experts from The Weather Channel selected the "Top Ten Storms of the Twentieth Century," the 1950 "Appalachian Storm" ranked eighth on the list. The blizzard, which struck during Thanksgiving weekend, claimed 278 lives, including 55 in Ohio. The storm shut down the Buckeye State as motorists abandoned 20,000 vehicles along Ohio highways.

Buckeye Blizzard tells the story of how the people of Ohio coped with the storm, which produced snowfalls of up to 40 inches and drifts exceeding 20 feet. Based on over 200 interviews and numerous newspaper accounts, the book includes chapters detailing the blizzard's effects on both cities and farms. The famous "Blizzard Bowl" game between Ohio State and Michigan is covered in another chapter, as are accounts of stranded motorists, ruined wedding plans, and births that became frightfully complicated.

ORDER YOUR COPY FOR $15, POSTPAID, FROM:

Pickenpaugh Books
501 Oaklawn Avenue
Caldwell, OH 43724

River on a Rampage:

The 1936 Flood from Chester to Marietta

In March 1936 a series of river floods devastated seventeen states and the District of Columbia. The waters left over one hundred people dead and damaged or destroyed nearly 35,000 buildings. Among the areas hardest hit was the Upper Ohio River Valley, where flood crest records, dating as far back as the 1700s, fell from Pittsburgh to Wheeling.

This is the story of how the people of Ohio and West Virginia dealt with one of the greatest natural disasters in the history of the valley. Based on eighty interviews and numerous newspaper accounts, *River on a Rampage* tells the stories of daring rescues, tragic deaths, and destruction on a wide scale. It also tells the story of how people came together to assist their neighbors and to clean up the mud and debris left behind by the receding waters.

ORDER YOUR COPY FOR $18, POSTPAID, FROM:

PICKENPAUGH BOOKS
501 OAKLAWN AVENUE
CALDWELL, OH 43724

SPECIAL OFFER:

ORDER BOTH *RIVER ON A RAMPAGE* AND *BUCKEYE BLIZZARD* FOR $23, A SAVINGS OF TEN DOLLARS.

The Forts of Ohio

By Gary S. Williams

Published by Buckeye Book Press

The earliest years of Ohio's recorded history were filled with conflict as Americans, Europeans and Native Americans struggled for control of the region. For the white intruders of this era, log forts became the key to survival in the wilderness. The story of these forts is the story of Ohio's beginnings and features some compelling tales.

At which Ohio fort:
- did one of the nation's most famous friendships begin when Lewis met Clark?
- did the officers write a Declaration of Independence that preceded the more famous one by 20 months?
- was a future president arrested for ordering a civilian to be given 50 lashes?
- did a besieged and starving garrison stampede their own relief convoy by firing their guns in celebration?
- was an American general, who was also a spy for Spain, suspected of trying to kill Anthony Wayne?
- did the commander name the post after his eleven-year old daughter?

Read about all of these and more in

THE FORTS OF OHIO,

the first directory of all the military stockades in Ohio.

ISBN 0-9703395-1-8. $19.00 plus $2.00 shipping/handling. Buckeye Book Press, 42100 Tp. Rd. 491, Caldwell, OH 43724. (740) 732-8169 or (740) 732-7291; e-mail: buckeye_books@earthlink.net